Satellite in Education

Satellite in Education
Critical knowledge Base for EDUSAT

Madhu Parhar

SHIPRA

First Published in 2006

Rs. 695

ISBN: 978-81-7541-267-5

2011 Impression

Satellite in Education

Published by:

SHIPRA PUBLICATIONS
LG 18-19, Pankaj Central Market,
I.P. Ext., Patparganj, Delhi 110092, India
Ph.: 011- 2223 5152, 2223 6152
Email: info@shiprapublication.com
www.shiprapublication.com

Dedication

Author's Royalty from this book is dedicated to the treatment of Cancer Patients

Foreword

Department of Space, ISRO, has taken India to a place of great repute in the world with the space programmes. In keeping with its dynamism, it was a momentous decision to launch a dedicated satellite for education. It is unique in the world. It is important to recognize the ambition and the confidence with which a dedicated satellite, with more than 70 channels, was conceptualized while we are still struggling to effectively utilize one dedicated channel for education. It is this quantum shift with the massive confidence that has made ISRO an enviable organization, anywhere in the world. The task of steering the dedicated satellite for education was the responsibility of Development and Educational Communication Unit of ISRO.

I had the rare privilege of being closely associated with the preparation of the concept document, organizing the national consultation in collaboration with DECU and preparing the project document, at the instance of Ministry of Human Resource Development, Government of India. It was during the involvement with the conceptualization and documentation of EDUSAT, particularly during projectization, I perceived the need to learn from related experiences from within the country, as well as from elsewhere. This perceived need inspired the creation of a critical knowledge base for satellite in education.

Obviously, development of a critical knowledge base on satellite in education was not an easy task. There are several

intricate issues, dimensions and concerns in use of 'Satellite in Education'. Use of satellite in education is spread all over the world; hence, the experience is extensive. On the other hand, there are large number of experiments on satellite based education of different complexities spread all over the world, including India. Beginning with the educational television in 1961-62 primarily to compensate the deficiencies in teaching of science and mathematics, India herself launched and experienced number of experiments with satellite in education like SITE experiment, classroom 2000 + experiment, interactive radio, interactive teleconferencing, etc. Also, such experiments threw up a large variety of important questions about the choice of technology, instructional design, content generation, software format, etc.

All these experiments involving large scale implementation of educational technology in general and media in particular, were backed by national policies from time to time. Such experiments at the micro as well as macro levels drew the attention of educational researchers. As a result, along with the field level experiences, there emerged number of research projects on the subject spread all over the globe during the last more than three decades. Research in educational media has been a strong trend among Indian educational researchers. Development of a comprehensive critical knowledge base demanded looking at all these various dimensions and much more.

I called upon Dr. Madhu Parhar, a competent and experienced researcher in educational media to undertake this difficult and arduous task of developing the critical knowledge base for satellite in education. She did a commendable work in this volume covering every important department of the subject of satellite in education. She has covered, in this book, history of satellite in education,

educational broadcasting and interactive television in addition to the international experiences on use of satellite in education and research in educational media. It is only with this comprehensiveness that this critical knowledge base becomes relevant, meaningful and useful to the policymakers, planners and managers of education. She deserves congratulation and special compliments for accomplishing this difficult task. I am happy to write this foreword to her book.

20th September, 2005 **Marmar Mukhopadhyay**
NIEPA, New Delhi

Acknowledgements

I was asked to take up this study by Prof. Marmar Mukhopadhyay when he was thick in the process of drafting the project document on EDUSAT. I had the great privilege of discussing with him and several other eminent scholars, specialist in information and communication technology, and administrators on EDUSAT. I also had the privilege of participating in the National Consultation on EDUSAT held jointly by DECU and NIEPA. Discussions with experts and participation in the National Consultation have helped me significantly in defining the parameters of my study.

I acknowledge all those who knowingly or unknowingly contributed to this study. My special thanks and appreciation is for Prof. Mukhopadhyay not only for imposing confidence on me and asking me to undertake the project, but also for guiding me all through out, and reviewing the manuscript again and again. I started working on this document in 2003, but had to stop for more than a year to take care of my ailing mother suffering from terminal cancer who finally left for her heavenly abode in August 2004; my second great loss, after I lost my father a few years earlier. Because of Prof. Mukhopadhyay's exhortations that I started working again on this book that is now ready to see the light of the day. I am grateful to him.

I am also thankful to all the authors from whom I have derived my critical knowledge base from internet and printed sources.

I appreciate the contribution of Shri Sabyasachi Panja for designing the beautiful and meaningful cover for this book. I have a fascination for his imagination and art work. I never miss an opportunity of approaching him, and he never fails me.

Shri Kalra went through the manuscript meticulously removing the howlers and improving the readability of the manuscript. I thank him.

Finally, I thank Shri D. Kumar of Shipra Publications for undertaking the publication so willingly and bringing it out within a very short time.

I hope my readers will find reading this book as worthy as I found labouring on this project for nearly two years.

5th September, 2005 **Madhu Parhar**
New Delhi

Contents

Contents

1

History of Satellite

Introduction

India has made significant strides in space technology and in its application in various areas. Activities in space technology in India started in early 1960s with the constitution of the Indian National Committee for Space Research by the Department of Atomic Energy in 1962. The first sounding rocket was launched in 1963 from Thumba Equatorial Rocket Launching Station (TERLS). Space Science and Technology Centre (SSTC) was established in 1965 in Thumba, followed by setting up of the Satellite Telecommunication Earth Station at Ahmedabad in 1967. The Indian Space Research Organization (ISRO) was created under the Department of Atomic Energy in 1969. ISRO played and continues to play the key role in planning and executing national space activities. In 1972, the Government of India established the Space Commission and the Department of Space (DOS). DOS conducts the nations space activities for ISRO.

The first Indian satellite Aryabhatta, named after the famous Indian astronomer, was launched in April 1975 by the erstwhile USSR Intercosmos Rocket into a near earth orbit. The credit for launching this first satellite goes to the vision of Dr. Vikram Sarahhai. This satellite carried out experiments in X-Ray Astronomy, Solar Physics and Astronomy. Next in line were Baskara I and II — experimental Earth Observation Satellites which were launched in June 1979 and November 1981, respectively. These two satellites were also put in space by Soviet Intercosmos Rocket of the erstwhile USSR. Both these satellites were experimental earth observation satellites.

Meanwhile, during 1977-79, the Satellite Communication Experiment Project (STEP) was conducted using the Franco-German Satellite "Symphonie". It provided experience in the operation of geostationary satellite system for domestic telecommunication and in designing and building ground infrastructure. The experience thus gained was instrumental for the inception of satellite communication technology in 1980 with the installation of seven earth stations.

Another experiment, Satellite Instructional Television Experiment (SITE) was conducted during 1975-76, which is one of the largest educational experiments using satellites. The experiment used USA's Application Technology Satellite (ATS-6). The details of the experiment are dealt with in Chapter Three.

In 1980, India successfully launched its own Rohini-I satellite on a Satellite Launch Vehicle (SLV) rocket from Sriharikota Island launch site.

In 1981, when Baskara II was launched, India also launched an experimental communication satellite, Ariane Passenger Payload Experiment (APPLE) with a C-Band transponder. It was launched by the Ariane Launch Vehicle of the European Space Agency (ESA). APPLE had large number of indigenous components, and 22 subsystems and was totally designed and fabricated in India. With APPLE, many communication experiments were carried out. APPLE gave a strong foundation to India for fixed satellite system, which led to the development of Indian National Satellite.

In the following pages, the history of various satellites launched by India so far is briefly described. There are many Websites which readers would like to visit for an in-depth knowledge and understanding of India's space programmes. Some of the sites are listed below:

http://www.spacetoday.org/India/IndiaSpaceSatellites.html

http://www.isro.org

http://www.itc.nl/~bakker/earsel/9806b.html

http://www.fas.org/spp/guide/india/bspace.html

Indian National Satellite (INSAT)

Indian National Satellite (INSAT) system is the result of the previous experiments like SITE, STEP and APPLE. It is one of the largest domestic communication satellite system, which includes eleven transponders. The first phase of INSAT programme was known as INSAT-1 series. There were problems with the INSAT-1 series satellites from the very beginning. When INSAT-1A was launched in 1982, it had to be abandoned within 147 days after its launch. INSAT-1B also had problems right from the beginning itself. INSAT-1C launched in July 1988 also had problems of solar power. INSAT-1D was launched in June 1990 from USA.

The second phase satellites of INSAT system were developed in India but launched by Ariane. The first in the second series was INSAT-2A, launched in July 1992. This was indigenously built multipurpose satellite. INSAT-2B was launched in July 1993 which was decommissioned from service in the same year. Two of its transponders were used for scientific experiments. It provided uninterrupted services in the areas of communication, television broadcasting, meteorology and distress alert. Next in the series was INSAT-2C which was launched in 1995 from KOUROV French Guyana. It provided mobile satellite services and business communication through KU band transponders. In 1997 INSAT-2D was launched. INSAT-2C and INSAT-2D, in addition to carrying communication transponders of INSAT-2A and 2B, incorporated KU band transponders for business communication, extended C band transponders to enable TV programme outreach beyond Indian boundaries catering to the population from South Asia to Middle East.

INSAT-2E was India's most advanced multipurpose communication satellite launched in 1999 by the European Ariane Rocket at KOUROV in French Guyana. This satellite weighted 2.5 tonnes and carried 17 transponders to provide 12,000 two-way links, or broadcast about 100 digitally compressed TV channels. The capacity of the INSAT was further expanded by the launch of INSAT-3B in the year 2000. Next in the INSAT-3 series was INSAT-3C.

The whole INSAT-3 series was aimed in achieving continuity of services, increased capacity and imported capability. The first four satellites in this series, 3A to 3D, were 2,500 kg satellites and were compatible with the Geostationary Satellite Launch Vehicle (GSLV), developed by ISRO. INSAT-3A to 3C emphasized on enhancing the telecommunication capabilities, whereas 3D emphasized on meteorological capabilities.

India has already planned and initiated INSAT-4 series of satellites. It is proposed that this series will have INSAT-4A to INSAT-4G with INSAT-4D as a spare. The transponders have been worked out after a detailed evaluation. It is expected that by 2007, INSAT will have 251 transponders in various bands. (www.isro.org/rep2002/links/Geostationary/html)

INSAT brought about a rapid expansion of the TV network and covered over 65 per cent of the Indian land mass and over 80 per cent of the total population. INSAT revolutionized telecommunication and TV broadcast in the country. More than 150 telecommunication terminals are today operating under INSAT network. INSAT network is also being substantially used for educational purposes, such as countrywide classroom programme conducted by the University Grants Commission (UGC), educational television programmes broadcast in local languages for the benefit of the rural population, and programmes broadcast by the Indira Gandhi National Open University (IGNOU). It is also being used in continuing education for industrial workers, training of block and village level extension and agricultural workers and farmers etc. INSAT, in addition provides radio networking.

The ground systems for the INSAT system are supplied by the Indian industry.

Indian Remote Sensing Satellites

India launched Remote Sensing Satellites IRS-1A in 1988 on board a Soviet 'Vostak" rocket. It was shut down for routine services after collecting about 300,000 images. IRS-1B was the follow-up satellite and was identical to IRS-1A. It was launched in 1991. IRS-P2 was launched by India's PSLV in 1994 and joined the IRS-1A and IRS-1B in enhancing the remote sensing services. In 1995, IRS-1C was put in space on board a Molniya rocket of Russia. IRS-1D, having similar capabilities as IRS-1C satellite was launched in 1997 by the Polar Satellite Launch Vehicle (PSLV); however, it was lost as it entered the wrong orbit due to a malfunction of the PSLV. The IRS-P series were considered to be experimental satellites. The focus of P series was on ocean chlorophyll, vegetation assessment, snow studies and geological mapping for identifying prospective mineral sites.

ISRO has at present more than ten remote sensing satellites under development, scheduled to be launched in the next decade. The data received from the IRS satellites were used in important applications, such as estimating agricultural crop acreage and yield, drought monitoring and assessment, flood mapping, land cover mapping, etc. Data from IRS satellites were received and processed by the National Remote Sensing Agency in Hyderabad. Twenty-two states have established remote sensing application centres. These centres carry projects as are relevant to their regions, besides participating in national level projects. With the IRS and INSAT series, India has started to get the benefits of space technology for developmental applications, specially in the areas of communication, broadcasting, meteorology, disaster management and management of resources.

The IRS-P4 series, known as OCEANSAT, was launched in 1999 to measure physical and biological oceanography parameters. The follow-up satellites in the IRS series are RESOURCESAT and CARTOSAT-1. RESOURCESAT is the state-of-art satellite and will be used for agricultural applications. CARTOSAT-1, which is an advanced cartographic satellite, has shown that India is a front-runner in the development and application of space based remote sensing. The CARTOSAT-1 and HAMSAT satellites were launched in May 2005 with the help of Polar Satellite Launch Vehicle. HAMSAT will provide ultra high and very high radio frequencies to broaden bandwidth.

Satellite Launch Vehicles

India has demonstrated its capability in the launch vehicle technology too. The first launch was done in 1980 using SLV-3. This launch vehicle placed the Rohini satellite into a near-earth orbit. In 1981 and 1983, two more launches of SLV-3 were conducted. The third and the fourth developmental launches-the Augmented Satellite Launch Vehicles (ASLV-D3 and D4) were launched from Sriharikota range (SHAR) in 1992 and 1994 respectively. Another achievement in field of launch vehicles was when the Polar Satellite Launch Vehicle (PSLV) was developed in 1993. However, it could not place the IRS-1E satellite on board. The second launch of PSLV-D2 (in 1994) and PSLV-D3 (in 1996) were successful. India became self-reliant in launch vehicle technology for launching the remote sensing and geostationary satellites with operationalisation of Geosynchronous Satellite Launch Vehicle (GSLV). GSLV rockets were blasted in the year 2001 from Sriharikota launch site and are capable to boost a large communications or weather satellite to a stationary orbit.

GRAMSAT

The concept of dedicated GRAMSAT satellites was developed, keeping in mind the need to eradicate illiteracy in rural areas. The GRAMSAT is to assist in providing continuing education for special groups to ensure that their skills (technical) are upgraded from time to time.

As part of a countrywide GRAMSAT pilot, Swaran Jayanti Vidya Vikas Antariksh Upagraha Yojana (Vidyavahini) has been inaugurated in Orrisa using INSAT-3B. This will provide developmental communication to about 800 villages in the Kalahandi – Bolangair-Koraput region. A transponder of INSAT-3B is also given to Andhra Pradesh for promoting distance education, telemedicine, agriculture extension, e-governance and community Internet centres. This pilot project will cover gradually other states also (Kasturirangan, 2003).

METSAT

India also launched METSAT in 2002 from Prof. Satish Dhawan Space Centre in Andhra Pradesh, which is an exclusive and dedicated meteorological satellite. The satellite has been built by ISRO and will support India's meteorological department by providing meteorological services from geostationary orbit. The services include cyclone warning, dissemination services, meteorological data collection, and weather imagery on a continuous basis. Before the launch of METSAT, the meteorological services were combined with telecommunication and TV services in INSAT spacecraft. METSAT will relay the data to the Meteorological Data Utilization Centre, New Delhi.

GSAT – Experimental Satellites

GSATs are experimental satellites. The first, GSAT-1, satellite was launched by GSLV-D1 flight in April 2001. It carried two S-band transponders for Digital Audio Broadcast (DAB) and three normal C-band transponders. It developed minor problems, which prevented to carry out experiments on board. The 1.54 metric tonne satellite was orbiting with a period of 23 hours two minutes, instead of planned 24 geosynchronous orbit. This satellite was to be used for a variety of experiments such as digital audio broadcasting and compressed digital TV signal transmission.

GSAT-2, which is another experimental satellite, was shot in space by indigenous rocket GSLV-D2 in May 2003 from Satish Dhawan Space Centre of Sriharkota. GSAT-2 caries four experimental payloads, four C-band transponders, two KU-band transponders and a Mobile Satellite service payload. Besides the communication service payloads, the GSAT-2 carries four piggy back experimental payloads like Total Radiation Dose Monitor, Surface Charge Monitor, Solar X-ray Spectrometer and Coherent Radio Beacon Experiment.

GSAT-3 and GSAT-4 are under planning. These satellites will carry regenerative transponders.

EDUSAT

Edusat, India's first thematic satellite dedicated exclusively for education, was launched from Satish Dhawan Space Centre in Sriharikota on September 20, 2004. The 1950-kg satellite, placed in the geosynchronous stationary orbit, has multiple regional beams covering different parts of the country. It has five Ku-band transponders with spot beam covering northern, northeastern, eastern, southern and western regions. It has one Ku-band transponder with its footprint covering the mainland and six other C-band transponders with national coverage beams. The Edusat satellite has been developed by ISRO and the payloads by the Space Application Centre, Ahemedabad. For the post launch operations, Master Control Facility at Hassan is responsible. ISRO took about three years to build the satellite at a cost of $17 million. The satellite has a mission life of seven years.

Dr. Kasturirangan, who was Chairman of ISRO at the conceptualization stage of Edusat said, "The satellite is being planned in view of the challenges faced by the nation in the field of education and the potential of using satellite communication to support education". Dr. Madhavan Nair, Chairman ISRO, at the launch of Edusat said, "India has proved that it can take satellite projects with perfection and thoroughness to meet any global standards. There is need to reach the remote parts of the country and provide literacy programmes and this can be achieved by Edusat".

A document "*Educating The Nation – Need for a Dedicated Satellite*" was prepared by Prof. Marmar Mukhopadhyay with input from experts from DECU, Ahmedabad. The document describes the challenges of Indian education and the various responses to these challenges. (Details of the contents of the document are already described in Chapter 2 by Prof. Mukhopadhyay in the *Story of EDUSAT*).

Pilot projects have been undertaken to ensure the effective utilization of Edusat. These are in Karnataka, Maharashtra and Madhya Pradesh, and constitute the first phase experiments. In the second and third phases, the Edusat network will be fully operational.

> Before the launch of Edusat in September 2004, ISRO used INSAT-3B for running three pilot projects. The projects were undertaken by Visvesvaraya Technological University (VTU) of Karnataka, the Yashwantrao Chavan Maharashtra Open University, Nasik, and Rajiv Gandhi Technical University in Madhya Pradesh. All the three universities were provided a studio from where the virtual class was taken. The lectures delivered were uplinked to the satellite and downlinked to the ground terminals.
>
> The VTU has 118 engineering colleges in Karnataka with more than 1.3 lakh students. In the pilot project, 100 colleges were given interactive systems and the others were provided with non-interactive reception sets. The response of the

students, especially in the remote areas, was good. The University felt that the pilot phase was useful in sorting out technical issues. The lectures were also made available on a CD.

A similar experiment was held at YCMOU. The university was given 100 reception terminals. Subject experts delivered lessons at the university headquarters in Nasik which were received by the students in the remote areas.

Conclusion

In the study of history of satellites, three major issues are of interest. These are the sequence of design and production of satellites, launching of satellites, and use of satellites for education. Although the history documented here is not exhaustive, the first satellite was designed and launched as early as in 1950s – about 50 years ago. The leaders were USA, Canada, UK and France, followed by Japan. Importantly, all these countries are industrially advanced and are developed. Two countries that belong to the elite six-nation club of satellite production and launching are China and India. The common attributes shared by these two countries are their large population, massive illiteracy, and wide spread poverty. These apparently is a contradiction in that such otherwise poor countries have taken to expensive and sophisticated space technology. Both India and China have drawn flak for such technology choice. Their choices can be dated back to nearly more than three and a half decades.

Looking back, one now appreciates the vision of Pandit Jawaharlal Nehru and Sri Vikram Sarabhai. It is because of such technology choice and development, space technology in particular, that India and China have been steadily interchanging their positions with the developed countries. In the centre-periphery paradigm, these two countries are increasingly becoming the centre, pushing the developed countries to the periphery. The space technology, particularly satellite design, development and launching, is not only expensive but also fraught with risk. One single failure in launching means sinking massive national resources. India faced such experience and dilemma. It is refreshing to experience that such failures have been made full use of to enrich the bouquet of learning, although these could have led to the development of feeling of helplessness and withdrawal. This determined approach has given the sophistication to achieve high order of success and confidence. The successful launch of educational satellite is being planned to be followed with a series of satellites that can support other development needs, particularly health. The most ambitious of course is the mission-moon.

History of satellite in the world, as much as in India, is exciting. Since this is an event located much more into the future, history is still to mature. It will unfold over the years. The history documented here is only the beginning of a long journey.

2

Committees, Policies and Plans

Introduction

Since Independence, India has made great strides in the field of education. The educational scenario in India is envisioned in its different educational policies that form the backbone of planned developments in education. Several committees and commissions have been set up from time to time since independence, the first being the University Education Commission, better known as Radhakrishnan Commission. It submitted its report in 1948. In 1952 came the report of the Secondary Education Commission, chaired by Sir Lakshmanswamy Mudaliar. The landmark and the most comprehensive report on education came from the Education Commission in 1966. The recommendations of their Commission became the basis for India's first National Policy on Education announced in 1968. Later, the Ministry of Education and Social Welfare, Government of India, prepared a draft National Policy on Education, 1979. But the most important event in educational policy making was the National Policy on Education in 1986 along with the *Programme of Action*. The National Policy recommended the review of the policy and progress of implementation every five years. Accordingly, a committee was appointed under the chairmanship of Shri Ramamurthy. Based on the report of this committee, the *Programme of Action* was revised in 1992.

University Grants Commission also have been appointing committees since 1961 to recommend ways and means of maintaining and improving the standards of tertiary education (Sidhanta Committee 1961, Mahajani Committee 1964, Gajendragadkar Committee 1971, Gnanam Committee 1990, and Rastogi Committee 1994). Out of these, only Sidhanta Committee undertook a systematic and objective investigation of problems relating to the standards of higher education in Indian universities. This committee recommended use of audio-visual aids, such as teaching machines, television, radio, films, and tape recorders, as in other parts of the world, for improving teaching in the universities. The committee proposed that agency like UGC must collect and communicate information about various teaching aids to the universities and colleges. The other committees did not mention anything about educational media. The Rastogi committee felt the need for improving the quality of education by teachers using educational technology. The report suggested that teachers must orient themselves, generate/prepare materials and convert them into programmed texts.

In this chapter, an effort has been made to analyze the recommendations of various committees and commissions to derive policy guidelines with respect to media in education.

University Education Commission

The University Education Commission (1948) dealt with the standards of teaching in the universities. Commission contended that the standards can be maintained by providing proper equipment, buildings, workshops, and technicians. There were no direct recommendations on educational media (*Ministry of Education 1950*).

Secondary Education Commission

The Secondary Education Commission (1952) examined the prevailing system of secondary education in the country and suggested measures for its reorganization and improvement, and described the place of visual aids in secondary schools. It reports that "the development of new types of visual aids provides unlimited possibilities for the pupils to obtain knowledge of the different stages of their educational ladder. Thus to broaden the scope of pupils' understanding, films must be available which not only depict the actual nature and conditions of work in a particular industry, but also supplement this with information concerning the daily routine of the worker on the job". The Commission felt that there was a need to prepare educational films that showed the status of industrial, agricultural, technical and other vocations. It pointed out that there were modern methods of audio-visual education being used in different countries, which had yet to be more fully utilized in our schools. It recommended that suitable provision must be made for such methods in the schools. The equipment mentioned in the report are: film and films strips, projectors, radios, magic lanterns and the epidiascopes etc. It was suggested that such appliances could be shared by two or three schools in rotation at different times of the day or on different days. Radio could help in giving general education to the students of schools and colleges and close liaison should be maintained between the teaching staff of the school and those connected with All India Radio

(Ministry of Education 1956). The Commission recommended radio as the mass media.

An interesting feature of this document is the concept of peripatetic media shared by 2/3 school's when in those days schools in rural areas were located at great distances from one another and transport system was grossly underdeveloped.

Keeping in view the recommendations made by the Secondary Education Commission that appropriate media should be used to stimulate the teaching-learning process, the first National Board of Audio-Visual Education was set up in 1952 to improve the quality of teaching-learning process. By 1959, the National Institute of Audio-Visual Education started functioning at the national level. Later on, both merged with the Department of Audio-Visual Aids, National Council of Educational Research and Training (NCERT). The first television centre was set up in Delhi in September 1959, as part of All India Radio.

Education Commission 1964–1966

The report of the Education Commission, popularly known as Kothari Commission, is divided into several chapters and one of the chapters "Teaching Method, Guidance and Evaluation" describes the use of media in education.

The Commission (Ministry of Education 1966) explains that in majority of schools, particularly at the primary stage, there is a total absence of basic equipment and teaching aids, such as a good Blackboard (BB), a small library, essential maps and charts, science apparatus and display material. Supply of these teaching aids to every school is essential for the improvement of the quality of teaching. The Commission recommended that lists of minimum teaching aids and equipment needed by each category of schools should be prepared, and as a first step, a good Blackboard should be provided to all the schools.

New techniques of teaching being used in the advanced countries were also suggested. The techniques involve large scale use of films, radios, tape recorders and other audio-visual aids, the introduction of open and close circuit television, the provision of language laboratories, programmed instructional methods, and simple and highly sophisticated forms of teaching machines. Films, film strips, etc., must be made available to every school complexes. Majority of upper primary and secondary schools should be equipped with low cost radio sets. Commission also recommended that education departments should collaborate with All India Radio for the use of radio lessons, to be supplemented with printed material for the teachers and for pupils. Broadcasting of special radio talks in the early morning or late evening, specially designed for teachers, would help enhance the subject knowledge of teachers and guide them in lesson preparation. The more sophisticated forms of newer techniques could be used only on an experimental basis and in few schools. The Commission observed that schools should use equipment that is in consonance with the level of technology in the society. Sophisticated equipment given to rural school, for instance, cannot be maintained and optimally utilized.

Majority the teachers must rely on inexpensive teaching equipment, which is easily available in the locality. Hence, for improving teaching in the schools, following programmes can be done:

- Training of teachers in the use and preparation of simple teaching aids,

- Manufacture of simple equipment on a large scale for reducing cost and its distribution to schools, and
- Sharing of the more costly equipment by schools in a given neighborhood.

As can be seen, even in 1968, choice, rather a limited choice, was radio with emphasis on localized modular media and low cost local material. Attention must also be paid to the Commission's alertness to new developments, e.g., close circuit television, programmed instruction and sophisticated teaching machines that have remained confined to white collar experiments in a few elite institutions even after four decades.

National Policy on Education, 1968

It was felt towards the end of the Third Five-Year Plan that a comprehensive review of the educational system with a view to initiating a fresh and more determined effort at educational reconstruction should be done. Hence, Education Commission was appointed to advise the government on the national pattern of education and on principles and policies for the development of education at all stages. The Commission's report was discussed thoroughly, and as a result a general consensus on national policy on education emerged. The National Policy on Education, 1968, envisaged a radical transformation of the education system in order to relate it more closely to the lives of the people, provide expanded educational opportunities, and initiate a sustained intensive effort to raise the quality of education.

The policy emphasized on the following principles (Ministry of Education 1968):

1. Free and Compulsory Education

2. Status, Emoluments and Education of Teachers
3. Development of Languages
4. Equalization of Educational Opportunity
5. Identification of Talent
6. Work Experience and National Service
7. Science Education and Research
8. Education for Agriculture and Industry
9. Production of Books
10. Examination
11. Secondary Education
12. University Education
13. Part-time Education
14. Spread of Literacy
15. Games and Sports
16. Education of Minorities and Educational Structure.

The NPE adopted in 1968 was based on the recommendations of the Education Commission (1964-66). Interestingly, NPE 1968 is silent on educational technology and media, though Education Commission made important recommendations on the issue. Yet, the development is worth noting.

For enhancing the efficiency of the education system as a whole and making it much more relevant to socio-economic need, an educational technology programme was started in the year 1972 in the central sector for widening access to and bringing out qualitative improvement in education. It included curriculum construction, preparation of audio-visual aids and their use in teacher training institutes for overall quality improvement in education.

With the above programme, a Centre for Educational Technology was set up in the NCERT in 1973 and 100 percent assistance was provided to twenty-one states for setting up ET cells.

National Guidelines for Educational Broadcasting, 1983

Ministry of Human Resource Development issued National Guidelines for Educational Broadcasting (NGEB) in 1983. The guidelines define the "Role of Educational Broadcasting" both for radio and television. It is, among other things, expected to act "as a major component of the non-formal education system, providing an alternative approach to the education of out-of-school children, youth and adults (NGEB, 1983). Further, universalization of elementary education for girls, rural and urban poor have been considered as areas of priority. NGEB states that "Educational Broadcasting should be integrated within the total educational system and the responsibility for policy and management of educational broadcasting should be with the educational authority".

The guidelines recommended taking "cognizance of localized needs, differences in language and culture and other similar phenomena be so organized that it can be regionalized and localized".

National Policy of Education, 1986

The NPE, 1968, led to considerable expansion of the educational facilities all over the country at all levels. Attention was paid to the creation of basic educational facilities in rural areas. Efforts were also initiated to adopt a common structure of education having a common scheme of studies.

However, the 1968 Policy did not get translated into a detailed strategy of implementation. Hence, the problems of access, quality, quantity, relevance and financial outlay accumulated over the years. To respond to these challenges, the new National Policy on Education (NPE) was adopted by the Government of India in 1986. The Ministry of Human Resource also prepared the Programme of Action (POA).

The policy document emphasized on media and use of educational technology in education.

From the NPE 1986, the following tasks emerged (MHRD 1986):

1. Expand the TV and Radio transmission network to:
   (a) Establish radio stations in teaching universities/ colleges during 7th plan
   (b) Provide a dedicated educational channel by 1991-92
   (c) Create a dedicated satellite system for educational needs in the long term.
2. Expand in-house programme production facilities to generate adequate capacity in major Indian languages by 1990.
3. Develop facilities/organizations for production, duplication and dissemination of curricular support material using non-broadcast methods.
4. Develop training programmes for manpower generation for educational media during the 7th Plan.
5. Provide radio receivers in all primary/elementary schools during the 7th Plan and TV sets to all schools by 1995.

6. Eliminate elements of consumerism, violence from media programmes.
7. Mount a technology mission to develop a reliable source of electric supply to schools in remote areas by 1990.

Based on the above tasks, the policy envisaged the following strategies:

1. Educational technology should reach out to the most distant areas and most deprived sections simultaneously with the areas of comparative affluence and ready availability. This approach will favour the use of broadcast methods over the non-broadcast methods. It is not possible to broadcast programmes for every class through radio and TV, coordinated with their teaching schedule, hence, radio and TV can be utilized effectively only for enrichment of the learning process and to transmit course material for distance education. It would be desirable that maintenance structures be decentralized. Video technology offers considerable potential for improving the quality of education especially at higher levels.
2. ET to reach to large numbers in remote and inaccessible areas. However, all that technology requires is supporting infrastructure like trained manpower, competent and willing teachers, school buildings, etc.

The policy document gives a brief description on the then situation on the use of technological aids for improving the quality of education. This includes the audio-visual and film libraries, Educational Technology cells in 21 States/UTs and a Centre of Educational Technology in the NCERT. It also describes the school radio broadcasts, curriculum based school TV programmes for secondary school, educational television of general enrichment for children, enrichment programme for university/college students.

The NPE, 1986, and its companion, POA led to the formulation of at least two major centrally sponsored schemes, namely Educational Technology Scheme and CLASS project to translate policy into action. A brief glimpse is given below:

> The Programme of Action led to the formulation of the Educational Technology Scheme and was initiated in 1987-88. The broad objective of the ET scheme was to strengthen both ETV and audio programme production capabilities and providing wider access to the same by supplying one lakh radio-cum cassette players to primary schools during the seventh plan. Under the scheme funds were released to 7 State Institutes of Educational Technology (SIET) in Andhra Pradesh, Bihar, Gujarat, Maharashtra, Orissa, Uttar Pradesh and Kerala.
>
> The scheme was divided into two phases – last three years of Seventh Five-Year Plan upto 1989-90, and 1990-91 of the Eighth Plan.
>
> The scheme had primarily three components. These were:
>
> - Development of infrastructures in educational technology institutions – CIET, SIET and ET cells,
> - Development of software, and
> - Provision of reception sets, colour television and radio-cum-cassette players.
>
> The Parliamentary Standing Committee on Human Resource Development in its 139th report on Demands for

Grants 2003-2004 of the Department of Secondary and Higher Education presented to the Rajya Sabha in April 2003, noted that the ET scheme was initiated in 1972 to increase access to education. Funds were released to SIETs for producing programmes for the school sector for telecast through Doordarshan and Akashvani. The report stated that during the Ninth Five-Year Plan, an amount of Rs. 34.83 crores was released and 3,509 audio/video programmes were produced by the SIETs and CIET. An amount of Rs 13.03 crore was released during the same plan period to provide 29,781 RCCPs and 8,826 TVs. The Committee reports that under the ET scheme the audio programmes made by SIET during the financial year 2001-2002 were only 51. These were less than the video programmes that were 789 in number. Committee took a serious note of the fact that the Department has spent so much of money during the Ninth Plan. The amount of Rs 47.86 crore was 61.67% of the total allocation (Rs 77.70 crore).

The Committee was informed that the Department has impressed upon the CIETs and SIETs to produce programmes which could be telecast on the fully dedicated educational channel Gyan Darshan.

Presently the two schemes-CLASS and ET have been merged.

Source: 139th Report of HRD, 2004.

The Educational Technology Scheme was evaluated at the initiative of Ministry of Human Resource Development in 3820 schools spread over 45 districts in 15 States and two Union Territories.

The objectives of this evaluative study were to:

- Assess the extent of utilization of RCCPs and CTVs provided to the elementary schools,

- Study the factors that either facilitate or retard utilization of media facilities,
- Find out the difficulties experienced by the principals and teachers regarding use of RCCP and CTV sets in their teaching-learning process, and
- Provide guidelines on management impact to improve media utilization in schools.

The evaluative study reveals that there is a wide disparity in the provision of facilities among the states, districts and the schools. No television sets were provided in the States of Assam, Haryana, Himachal Pradesh, Karnataka, Maharashtra, Manipur, Mizoram, Nagaland, Punjab and Tamil Nadu, while Andhra Pradesh, Gujarat, Madhya Pradesh, Mizoram, Orissa, Uttar Pradesh, Chandigarh and Delhi have been provided with both TV and RCCPs.

As far as infrastructural positions of these schools are concerned, North East region needs attention where the condition of school buildings, classroom facilities and electricity supply are in a poor state. Unless these are developed, media can never be successfully utilized. But the case of Andhra Pradesh, Gujarat, Karnataka, Madhya Pradesh, Maharashtra and Orissa are strong enough to promote Educational Technology and Media. Most of these states have all weather buildings with better electricity supply position.

Special attention needs to be given to develop remote and under-developed areas of the country to increase access to education and improve teaching-learning. Educational Technology Scheme is a critical input for these areas and investment can be augmented. Developed areas can be taken as a model for innovations and experiments for other States to follow.

Success of the ET Scheme depends on the preparedness and orientation of the teachers to successfully implement the scheme in their schools. Out of 3820 schools surveyed in the project, there are only 631 teachers found to have undergone some orientation training in media.

Out of this, Andhra Pradesh has maximum number of teachers. Next in order is Punjab, and Delhi. Percentage of teachers trained in media is low in the States of Uttar Pradesh, Tamil Nadu, Orissa, Karnataka and Arunachal Pradesh.

Main objective of media implementation was based on the assumptions to increase the access to education as well as enhance the standard of education in the rural areas. Not only the teachers, but also their qualifications and training are important considerations.

The utilization of media can substantially improve if:

- Teachers receive the information chart or broadcast schedule so that they can introduce the topic and prepare the children to listen or view a programme.
- Broadcast is included in the school timetable.
- Teachers maintain a logbook on use of sets.
- Teachers are trained to discuss the programme with the children.

Principals and teachers were asked to give reasons for not exposing the educational TV or radio programmes in their schools. Their reasons varied from state to state depending on the availability of room, teacher, electricity, relevance and usefulness to the students. Andhra Pradesh schools were unable to expose the programme because most of the sets were out of order. In Assam and Mizoram, teachers are engaged in various other programmes and cannot spare time for its exposure and maintenance. Gujarat, Maharashtra, Manipur, Tamil Nadu and Chandigarh schools expose only the relevant and useful programmes to the children. The schools of Karnataka, Punjab, Chandigarh and Delhi do not receive the information/chart on the programmes in their schools. In its absence, they find it difficult to incorporate the media programmes in the timetable. Inadequate space has been the main reason for not telecasting or broadcasting the programmes in Orissa.

In the year 1989, the Ministry of Human Resource Development set up a group to study the use of Satellite Services for Education. The convener of the group was Kiran Karnik with eight other members. The groups presented the final report to the education secretaries with the following recommendations (Report 1989):

1. A need for full-fledged educational channel.
2. A new network of TV and radio transmitters be set up to take care of the broadcast time.
3. Action be initiated to reserve and augment satellite capabilities to meet the ETV requirements.
4. Adequate software production and training facilities must be set up.
5. Suitable organizational structure should be created to operate successfully the components of the ETV system.

Ramamurti Committee

In 1990, the Government of India appointed a committee to review the National Policy on Education, 1986. Acharya Ramamurti was appointed the chairman of the committee. The terms of reference of the committee were:

- To review the NPE 1986 and its implementation,
- To make recommendations regarding the revision of the policy, and
- To recommend action necessary for implementation of the revised policy within a time frame.

Chapter 12 of the report on "Content and Process of Education", deals with Educational Technology in NPE 1986. The Committee NEP 1986 – A Revision recommended that the Government should review the Educational Technology Programme as a whole. It should review specially the following:

1. Status of utilization of RCCPs and TVs provided to various states must be studied in detail so that their proper utilization is ensured. Where it is obvious that these equipment cannot be used, they should be transferred to schools where the infrastructure exists. The TV programmes cannot be substitute for normal teaching. Priority should be for use of audio and videocassettes for educational purposes. The reason is that the teachers will have the facility of playing them in a regulated way at the time they consider suitable for the students.
2. Within the Education Department, the monitoring of the implementation of this programme, should be in close coordination between the Schools Bureau and the Elementary Education Bureau, which is responsible, and deals with the problems of children of the relevant age group. Use of education technology hardware as well as software should be made part of monitoring of Universalisation of Elementary Education (UEE).

3. Teacher training programmes must provide for the use of this equipment. Training must emphasize on instructional designs suitable to local needs. Techno aids should be made available to the teachers only if and when needed.
4. Infrastructure and capability are available in existing institutions for the production of educational software in our country. The University Grants Commission (UGC), NCERT, CIEFL, Central Institute of Indian Languages (CIIL) and Kendriya Hindi Sansthan are the organizations that have facilities and relevant experiences. Creation of educational media foundation is worthwhile, but the government should lay down the modalities of utilizing the existing institutions.
5. Immediate steps should be taken for properly manning the technical and professional posts in the State Institutes of Educational Technology so that their capacities are utilized.
6. Early steps must be taken for implementing the programmes to have a channel of the Doordarshan dedicated for education. Doordarshan has been demanding commercial rates for telecasting educational programmes; it is not appropriate to apply commercial rates for educational programmes. The government must fund the costs involved, Information & Broadcasting Ministry meeting the capital cost, and the running cost being met by the Department of Education, MHRD on no loss, no profit basis.

Programme of Action, 1992

The Chapter on "Media and Educational Technology" in POA 1992 acknowledges the potential of modern communication technology, the NPE, 1986, and POA 1986 had spelt out. The Chapter describes the present situation of electronic media in different sectors like school, adult, higher, technical and primary education and teacher training (MHRD 1992). The POA 1992 explains the revised strategy and programmes in which efforts will continue for securing a reasonably large and fixed time slot on radio for transmission of educational programmes. Regarding TV, efforts have to continue for securing a dedicated channel for educational transmission. Simultaneously, emphasis must be laid on improving the quality of educational programmes and for optimum utilization of transmission facility. Following measures can be taken for this:

- The remaining SIETs would be made autonomous. Production facilities in North East will be set up.
- In SIETs association of professionals on deputation/ contract will be encouraged to professionalise the working environment.
- Professional talent would be associated through commissioned programmes.
- The EMRCs and AVRCs would be converted into autonomous departments of the university concerned and these institutions would associate professional talent from outside on contract basis. One new AVRC would be set up in each of the remaining larger states during the 8th Plan.

The UGC would set up adequate master's level courses or post-graduate diplomas in various aspects of educational programme production.

Viewing of programmes by large number of students

have obvious problems, both in terms of management and learner outcome. Following measures can be taken to enable more and more students to have access to educational programmes:

- Provision of receiving sets, RCCP and TV sets in large number of primary schools/upper primary schools.
- Production of programmes for upper primary sector
- Special efforts for production of recorded audiocassettes by CIET/SIET to ensure optimal utilization of RCCPs.
- Augmentation of equipment in SIET/CIET.
- Encouragement of educational institutions to raise resources locally to provide electronics hardware, radio, cassette player, TV and VCR
- Marketing of educational cassettes by the Inter University Consortium for Educational Communication (IUCEC).
- Development of IUCEC as the nodal agency for marketing of educational software.
- Setting up of training facilities for technical personnel by CIET and IUCEC on regional basis.
- Development by the IGNOU of a large range of recorded audio and audio-visual cassettes to support its various distance education courses.

The plan emphasizes the in-service training of teachers through TV and radio. The programme of continuing education would be given more support through Vivek Darpan and other such programmes and awareness for literacy would continue to be built up through capsules on the TV/Radio.

National Action Plan

Since Independence, Government of India is committed towards the universalisation of education. This is emphasized in all the policies and plan documents on education. During the Jometien Conference (1991), the Delhi Declaration (1993) and the mid decade review by the EFA Forum in Amman in 1996, India reaffirmed its resolve for universalisation of education. To achieve universalisation, a number of schemes and policies were implemented. Importance was given to quality of schools, specially the quality of teachers. It was felt that to optimize the teacher quality, continuous in-service education be imparted to teachers. The National Action Plan (NAP) on In-service Education of Primary Teachers through Distance Education, developed in 1996, was an initiative towards this objective. The Plan was funded by Asian Development Bank and promoted by UNESCO, New Delhi. The Plan was drafted by Prof Marmar Mukhopadhya under the overall advice of a National Advisory Committee.

The aim of the Plan was to provide an institutional framework for in-service education and sustainable renewal of primary teachers and capacity building of the system through interactive distance education. In more specific terms, the goals as mentioned in the Plan are (UNESCO 1996):

- Build capacity of the system for providing sustainable in-service education to primary teachers;
- Design and develop courses and programmes that are adaptable to local needs;
- Provide short in-service training to all qualified primary teachers once in a year;
- Upgrade all unqualified primary teachers by the end of ninth plan;

- Provide short term training to all teacher trainers;
- Provide short term training to all supervisory staff at least once on two years;
- Improve capability of training institutions involved;
- Establish a training network linking national, regional, state, district and block level centres for training delivery through distance education; and
- Improve inter-institutional linkages for greater effectiveness.

The academic focus in the Plan was on content and on training methodology. To maintain quality, it was proposed in the Plan to use a multi-channel delivery of education, with a combination of Printed Self Instructional Material, Personal Contact Programme, television and radio and internet. The multi-channel learning shall comprise the following:

1. Home Based Learning
   (a) Printed Self Instructional Material
   (b) Textual Material
   (c) Enrichment Reading – Magazines
   (d) Radio and Television Lessons
2. Site Based Learning (School and Workplace)
   (a) Action Research
   (b) Group Problem Solving
   (c) Field work
   (d) Experimentation
3. Center Based Learning (Block Level Resource Centre)
   (a) Lectures
   (b) Tutorials

(c) Group Discussions
(d) Video Aided Instruction
(e) Computer Assisted Learning
(f) Interactive CD-ROM

4. Institute Based Learning (DIET, SCERT etc)
(a) Lectures
(b) Tutorials
(c) Group Discussions
(d) Interactive Television
(e) Interactive CD ROM

The Plan indicates that the technology required for programme delivery is an important and sensitive issue. The lessons in this training will be delivered through either terrestrial or satellite modes. The main proposition of the NAP is to set up a digital interactive television network connecting all state headquarters (SCERTs) with the national headquarters through a mesh network and all districts (DIETs) through a star network during the IX Plan. The network is to extend to the block level connecting all BRCs during the X Plan.

National Action Plan now finds a place in the revised scheme of teacher education for the tenth Plan. A pilot project is proposed to train teachers through distance mode using interactive technology (*www.education.nic.in/html*).

National Curriculum Framework Review, 2005

The National Focus Group on Educational Technology of the National Curriculum Framework Review has fourteen members. There were other nine guest members who presented their views/experiments related to educational technology. The group members visited several innovative programmes. The draft position paper in the beginning has described the historical perspective of educational technology in the country. The group felt that the term ET is construed differently in different programmes and by different agencies. Initiatives taken in the voluntary sector, which enhances learning, are described. Similarly, the efforts made by the Government (SITE, INSAT, PMOST, SOPT, CLASS Etc) are presented. The successes and failures of the various schemes and programmes are listed. The focus group felt that an important lesson learnt is 'whether one uses low technology or high technology or micro or macro models, ET solution to educational problems is a matter of total fix'. Education must take recourse to the discipline of ET in organizing education, as the challenges faced by the country today are more grave than before. The features of the changing society are knowledge explosion, technological explosion, population explosion, and homogenization of the world and scarcity of resources. To address these problems the ET focus group laid down the following proposal for actions (NCERT 2005);

Reusing Programmes for Interactivity

There are number of institutions at the school, higher and national levels who have produced excellent programmes which are of good quality. These programmes must be identified and dubbed in different languages and reused. All the institutes that produce programmes must come under a network.

Information Collection

Institutions are not assigned any function for programming or collecting data in respect of innovations or assessment.

Any institution at the district level could consider taking up this role. There has to be inbuilt interactivity and data on programming needs to be collected.

Using Satellite, DTH and Other Technologies

India has launched a dedicated satellite 'Edusat' for education. It will reach the backward areas and marginalised populations and would enable a new type of programming that is better than disseminative programming. The DTH technology is another possibility to provide a channel for community television in different languages. All these resources must be utilised which will provide large scale access to all sections of children, even to out-of-school and the disabled.

The focus group has given certain specific proposals for school system. The group felt that special attention be given to continuing education of in-service teachers. The suggestions given are:

Revitalising and Reorienting Existing Resources

Country must use the services/facilities of existing institutions, trained professional and creative manpower in the area of ET. Institutions must have new roles like action research, data collection, training of teachers, developing models for interactive classes, tele and video conferencing etc. Teachers, parents and children at every level can generate materials.

Systemic Reforms

Reforms are achieved by ensuring opportunities for autonomous content generation by diverse communities. Focus must shift from fixed curriculum to flexible curricula,

ET be developed to enhance open education and transforming all schools into ICT rich environments.

Refreshing Skills of In-service Teachers

A system be created of life long professional development and support for leaders and managers and encourage ICT literacy to build comfort and later creativity in educational work.

Pre-service Teacher Education

Teachers should be introduced to flexible models of reaching curriculum goals and media and technology related methods of learning be introduced.

Research

A framework must be created to identify the generic skills needed for the new initiatives to be taken in ET.

The draft document of the focus group on Educational Technology misses out on the conceptual development of educational technology which includes the systems approach, instructional design, classroom transaction, learning assessment etc. The group has equated and dealt with media only. The latest literature explains Educational Technology differently (Mukhopadhyay, 2004). The purpose of educational technology is optimizing human learning, implying economics of learning'.

Conclusion

Recommendations of the committees and commissions provide the basis for educational policy formulation. Educational policies provide the direction for educational development. Hence, educational policy plays the most critical role in visioning education and the society; and also in shaping structures, contents, and processes of education. India witnessed, since independence, appointment of a number of committees on education both at the national and state levels. There have, however, been only three commissions, the last and the most comprehensive commission being forty years ago, i.e. the Education Commission (1964-66). During the 58 years of Indian independence, national policy enactments have happened only twice. First policy was enacted after 21 years of independence; and the second policy after another eighteen years. India has spent 19 more years since the formulation of the second national policy on education.

There are serious implications and meanings in this wide gap between appointment of commissions and enactment of policies. Most important is the lack of resilience of the system. The fast developments and changes in the structure of knowledge, the understanding of human learning, and changing socio-demographic characteristics of the society to be accommodated in a framework developed more than two decades ago is well nigh impossible. Logically, it is necessary to review and make fresh policy statements every five to six years as contemplated in NPE 1986. The second point of attraction is policy studies in education and educational media. There is a wide gap between the developments in educational media and policy statements, including recommendations of the committees and commissions. For example, educational radio broadcast began in 1930s in India. Yet, it did not find a mention in the Secondary Education Commission or even in the Education Commission or in the first National Policy on Education in any significant manner. The statements on educational technology and media in the first and second policy of education are peripheral, certainly not as the major instruments for achieving educational objectives.

The POA, following the NPE 1986, and still later, also do not provide any significant coverage to educational media. The ICT schemes of the government that comes closest to official policies and programmes are still to recognize certain important ICT tools for education, namely Internet for learning although this has been extensively debated and comprehensively reported in USA, Canada, UK and Australia.

Just as educational policies treat media and technology as a peripheral subject, it finds an interesting reflection in the policies in media and IT also. Here, education occurs as a peripheral subject. For example, education is missed out in the Planning Commission's document on India as a Knowledge Superpower. Similarly, in the Government of India's IT policy and media policy, education as a sector finds a very weak mention. It is possible to conclude that media and educational technology are still to find a focused attention and adequate policy support which may only be possible without greater understanding of the potential of educational technology and media in achieving social and individual goals of education.

3

Educational Broadcast

Television

Introduction

Educational mass media has been one of the major issues in contemporary world education. In USA and Europe, the radio and television has been extensively used for more than 50 years now. Its effects on the younger generation, and the old ones, have been studied in great details. *John Goodlad* (1983) in his book 'A Place Called School', points out that the television over a period between 1960 and 1980, moved from 8th place to 3rd out of 10 in terms of influencing the youth aged 13 to 19 years. *Marie Winn* (1983) in her book 'Children Without Childhood' acknowledges that the television is an enormously powerful, hypnotic form of entertainment. She further warns that the parents have little chance of controlling their child's exposure to every variety of human brutality and violence. *Deodhar* (1991), in his book wrote, "Television is often condemned as an Idiot Box. But this is no Idiot Box. It is a double-edged weapon. It can be the healing knife of a surgeon or a stabbing weapon of a killer. Power of media and its manipulative nature or its inexhaustible appeal to children is so unique that some studies have indignantly labeled it as a *Third Parent*".

Educational mass media had its origin practically during World War-I. British Broadcasting Company (BBC) was the first to begin school broadcasting in 1924. The BBC programmes gained great popularity as the radio could reach a large audience simultaneously with ease and at not much cost. Japan introduced school broadcasting in 1931, followed by Australia and New Zealand in 1932. India is no exception.

In this chapter, an effort has been made to trace the history of educational television and document some of the major television broadcast experiments in India. A brief description is also made on educational radio.

Educational Radio in India

The first radio programme in India was broadcast in 1923 by Radio Club of Bombay. The Indian Broadcasting Company was set up in Bombay on July 23, 1927. In the same year, Calcutta and Bombay were among the first radio stations to start school broadcasts though occasional in nature. All India Radio (AIR) began its operations formally in 1936. When India became Independent, the AIR network had only six stations located at Delhi, Bombay, Calcutta, Madras, Lucknow and Tiruchirapally. During 90s, there were around 141 broadcasting stations and several relay centres located in different parts of India. Today, AIR has 215 radio stations. There are 144 MW transmitters, 54 SW transmitters and 139 FM transmitters. With these infrastructure facilities, the present radio coverage in India is 91.37 per cent by area and 99.13 per cent by population *(www.allindiaradio.org)*. As many as 44 stations produce educational programmes in one form or the other and for one or the other level of learners.

As mentioned earlier, school broadcasting began in

Bombay as early as 1929, followed by Madras in 1930. The Calcutta station of AIR first broadcast school programmes in November 1932. But, these were informal and sporadic ventures. School broadcasting began in right earnest in 1938. In 1939, all AIR stations were asked to prepare school programme schedules in collaboration with the state education authorities. Two to five programmes of 20 to 30 minutes' duration each were transmitted each week and were directed to juniors (11 to 13 years) and seniors (14 to 16 years). The emphasis was on providing enrichment programmes or programmes on general knowledge to a large student audience.

The thrust and type of educational broadcasts for the secondary schools vary from state to state; these are mostly syllabus-based, and the subjects covered in these programmes are English, Regional Language, Science, Social Studies and Sanskrit. These programmes aim at helping the students and the teachers to update the content knowledge. These programmes. also expose the teachers to new approaches and methods of teaching. In order to break away from the stereotyped themes and topics, a few programmes on topics not in the syllabus are also broadcast. These fall in the category of enrichment programmes. About 70,000 Indian schools benefit from this service.

There is no central planning and production of educational programmes The educational radio programmes are planned and produced at the AIR stations in the respective language of the region. The School Broadcast Panels, attached to the AIR stations, advise on the programmes and programme schedules. The State Education Departments are represented on the panels. But only a small percentage of schools in a few states, such as Maharashtra, Tamil Nadu, and Jammu and Kashmir, have made arrangements for the students to hear these programmes under supervision. The arguments put forward by the educational authorities are that the school time-table is over-burdened; it is impossible to find time for accommodating these radio lessons. Because of this, the AIR introduced programmes for the primary classes on the assumptions that there would be more time available and greater flexibility possible at this stage of education.

Besides the regular educational broadcasts, there have been several major experiments in the use of radio in education. These experiments indicate that radio broadcast has been used either regularly or on project basis for all the levels of education. Under the joint auspices of the Department of Women and Child Development, NCERT and AIR, the Children's Enrichment Experiment Radio (CHEER) was launched on 2nd October 1992 for pre-school children in the age group 3-6 years. The programmes for primary education were introduced to reduce the dropout rate and enrich educational quality. Over the years, primary education has received a high priority in radio broadcast. AIR lays considerable emphasis on the planning and production of science programmes in both the formal and non-formal spheres of educational broadcasts. Special science cells have been set up in most of the major stations of the country to improve the quantity and quality of science programmes. These programmes include both syllabus-based as well as popular enrichment science programmes.

During the SITE experiment in 1975-76, in-service education in science was organized with the help of a multi-media package consisting of radio programmes as an important component. This was developed by the Centre for Educational Technology (CET), and was implemented in six SITE states. About 43,000 teachers of primary schools benefited from this programme.

Radio broadcast also serves the needs of the tertiary or university students through an enrichment service, which comprises a youth programme and radio support to the distance learners by the Delhi, Punjab, Madurai and Kashmir stations. AIR also provides broadcast support to the students of the Indira Gandhi National Open University (IGNOU). The broadcast started in collaboration with AIR stations of Mumbai, Hyderabad and Shillong in 1992. Shillong discontinued later. The target groups of this project were students of open universities.

Besides the formal system, radio broadcast has also provided significant support to the *National Adult Education Project* in order to remove illiteracy from the country. *Farm Schools* is another example of non-formal education through AIR. This was inaugurated in 1973 and thousands of farmers registered for different courses under this service.

Besides these, there are programmes for the teachers and the teacher educators. These programmes are intended to familiarize them with the methods of teaching, curricular changes and content advancement. This service has been necessitated on account of changes in school curriculum and methodology, particularly in subjects like Science, Mathematics, Social Studies and English. The radio has also been used for the teaching of mother tongue as the first language in Jaipur. The project (Radio Pilot Project) started in 1979 and lasted for four years. The aim of the project was to teach Hindi to school children in 500 primary schools of Jaipur and Ajmer districts of Rajasthan. Evaluation of the project showed improvement in the achievements of children. Hence, it was repeated in Hoshangabad district of Madhya Pradesh.

Community radios are another event where members of

the community get together and design, produce and air the programmes. The communities consist of several families, neighborhood or even several villages. In India, community radios are not common but a few initiatives were taken in various states. Some of the experiments like Kunjal Pachaee Kutch ji (in Kutch district of Gujarat), Chala Ho Gaon Mein (in Palamau district of Jharkand), Namma Dhwanj (in Kolar district of Karnataka) etc. have been successfully implemented. In all these experiments, the target groups were the villagers and the focus was on empowerment of women.

> Gyan Vani, the educational FM radio channel of India was launched in November 2001. It operates through several FM stations from various parts of the country. At present there are 17 FM stations operating from Allahabad, Bangalore, Bhopal, Chennai, Coimbatore, Delhi, Guwhati, Jabalpur, Kolkata, Lucknow, Mumbai, Mysore, Raipur, Rajkot, Shillong, Visakhapatnam, and Varanasi. This network will expand to a total of 40 stations in the near future. The Gyan Vani FM station broadcasts over a radius of 70 kms and hence has the capacity to be specific, catering to the educational and developmental needs of the locality. The broadcasts are in English, Hindi and the local language of the region. The local resource persons conduct the programmes and the duration varies from station to station. The programmes are contributed by various ministries, educational institutions, NGOs, national level institutes like IGNOU, NCERT, UGC etc.
>
> Feedback from the audiences of Gyan Vani station by *Usha Chander and Sharma* (2003) found that the learners prefer discussion based programmes followed by quiz programmes. Learners felt the need of interactivity in the Gyan Vani programmes.
>
> *Source: EMPC IGNOU, June 2005.*

Educational radio broadcasts have not only a long and variegated history but are rich with wide spectrum of experiments and experiences. Broadcasting is used for teaching in schools, colleges and in non-formal education. It is evident from the above description that radio programmes are used for large-scale audiences and received free of charge by any listener.

Educational Television Broadcast

Educational television had an interesting beginning in India. The first experimental TV service was launched in India on 15 September 1959 to produce and transmit social education programmes. UNESCO provided 70 TV sets for community viewing and some portable generator sets for experimenting with TV in some of the selected villages where there was no electricity. To begin with, 66 tele-clubs were established by All India Radio in collaboration with the Directorate of Education, Delhi Administration. In1960, the Ford Foundation conducted a survey of the then existing condition and studied the feasibility and scope of future developments of educational television in India and received necessary equipments for strengthening television services in Delhi. In the decade beginning 1961, India passed through difficult times, and economic recession was high. There was no extension of TV during this period. After 12 years, a second TV centre at Bombay was inaugurated in 1972. Delhi Doordarshan started its general service in 1965 and a special service called *Krishi Darshan* was launched in 1966 with the objective of promoting rural reconstruction and orienting the rural masses in modern scientific methods of farming. Initially the programme was telecast daily for two hours and fifteen minutes only. In 1973, Pune TV relay station was set up. Srinagar Doordarshan was the third Kendra that appeared on Doordarshan map in 1973. The next was in Amritsar. TV centres started functioning in Calcutta and Madras in 1975. The introduction of TV in several states of India was a great turning point in the history of education of the country. SITE experiment was started in 1975. In 1976, Doordarshan was bifurcated from AIR and became a separate department of the Government of India. INSAT was launched in 1982. Another landmark was the beginning of colour TV/telecast. Doordarshan gave wide coverage to Asian Games in 1982 through its 21 low power transmitters. National programme was also started in 1982 for one and half hours. The morning transmission was introduced in 1987 initially for a period of 45 minutes daily. The afternoon transmission was initially introduced in 1989 and was only on Sundays. Another landmark in the Indian television was the introduction of satellite based services.

At present, Doordarshan, which is the national broadcaster, operates 25 channels through different satellites. These are DD-1, DD-2, DD-Sports, DD-Bharti, DD-World, Gyan Darshan, State Networks and Regional Language Channels.

There are a number of private television channels also. Among these, Zee TV was the first private channel to start educational telecast in 1995. It is called Zee Education (ZED), and has over the time evolved into a full-fledged channel.

With this brief history of the development of television particularly educational television in India, let us review some major experiments in educational television.

School Television in India

All India Radio's experimental television service was inaugurated on 15 September 1959. On this day, India joined other Asian nations having television service of its own. The project was for experimentation, training and evaluation. Programmes of educational and cultural value were for both urban and rural communities and were also of interest to school students.

Once the planning for general programmes and school series commenced, Ford Foundation was approached for assistance in the development of educational television. On 19 January, 1961, AIR, in collaboration with Directorate of Education, Delhi, started a weekly series of specially designed programmes for Class IX students of higher secondary schools. Ford Foundation provided practical support for a period of four years for educational television for Delhi schools.

Regular transmission started in October 1961, with three lessons per week in Physics and Chemistry and one lesson per week in English and Hindi for Class IX. In the following year one lesson each in Physics, Chemistry, English and Hindi were introduced for Class X, and the frequency of Physics and Chemistry lessons for Class IX was reduced to two lessons per week. Later in 1962, English and Hindi lessons were dropped in view of the state of emergency in the country leading to mounting pressure on telecast time. English lessons were introduced for Class VI in 1963 as it was felt that television lessons in English would be more useful and effective in the middle classes as students start learning English in that class.

Telecast of English lessons was extended to Class VII and Physics and Chemistry lessons to Class XI in 1964-65. The programmes on Current Affairs were replaced by programmes on International Cooperation and were coordinated with the syllabus of Social Studies for Class VIII. During the year 1985-86, English lessons were extended to Class VIII and

General Science to Classes VII and VIII. Workshops were organized for orienting classroom teachers and principals; and to involve them in planning and development of the project.

School television enabled all students to benefit equally from talented teachers, properly equipped labs and appropriate audio-visual aids and their use. Subjects where there was paucity of facilities in schools were chosen for school television programmes. Physics and Chemistry were selected as principal subjects because majority of the teachers were ill-equipped for teaching of science. Guidance notes were supplied to the teachers in advance since classroom teachers had to play an important role during the transmission. Teachers were asked to make sure that students were not just passive viewers by involving them in discussions and to try and gauge the extent of achievement of the predetermined objectives.

During 1967-68, the frequency of lessons remained the same but in the next year lessons in Social Studies were added. In the year 1970-71, lessons in Mathematics for Class VI were added and one Physics lesson for Class X was replaced by one Biology lesson for the same class.

In 1971-72, Physics for Class XI was taken off and programmes in Mathematics for Class VII were introduced. Social Studies for Class VIII was replaced by that for Class VI.

In 1974-75, there were some changes in the schedule of TV lessons for Class XI; Chemistry lessons were telecast during the first half and in the second half, lessons in Physics were telecast.

With the introduction of 10+2+3 scheme in 1975-76, Physics and Chemistry lessons were reintroduced for Class XI as the syllabus was revised and teaching needed updating. In 1976-77, there were no television lessons for Class XI. As

Class X came under 10+2+3 scheme that year, Physics lessons both for Classes IX and X were telecast regularly every week. In the 1978-79 session, there was no change in programmes for secondary stage and the pattern continued till 1983-84. TV lessons for teachers known as 'Teachers Training Programmes' which were there till 1983-84, were dropped the next year.

A separate television branch in the Directorate of Education, Delhi, was created in 1967 in view of the expansion of the project and to meet expanding number of programmes needed. Presently, school television programmes have been discontinued.

Satellite Instructional Television Experiment (SITE)

It was the largest communication experiment in the use of satellite in support of developmental and educational programmes in modern times. The main impetus for the SITE project came from Prof. V. A. Sarabhai.

In 1969, India and USA started an experiment called SIET by means of Applications Technology (ATS-6). On May 30, 1974, the Satellite was launched from Cape Carnival in USA. The telecast via this satellite began in India from August 1, 1975. Indian Space Research Organization (ISRO) with All India Radio (AIR) took the responsibility of broadcasting ETV programmes to the selected villages in six states of Andhra Pradesh, Bihar, Karnataka, Orissa, Madhya Pradesh and Rajasthan, selected on the basis of their educational backwardness.

The experiment continued from August 1975 to July 1976. The instructional objectives of SITE were in the fields of education, agriculture, health and family planning and national integration.

About 2400 Direct Reception Television Sets (DRS) deployed for SITE were located in different cultural, linguistic and agricultural regions of the country. Different socio-economic environments were also chosen for the purpose. Television broadcasts via satellite were made available for four hours a day, one and half hour in the morning and two and half hours in the evening. Morning times were utilized for broadcasting programmes for children which were enrichment programmes for the age group 5 to 12 years; evening programmes were directed to adults.

SITE covered four different language regions but children of other regions also watched these programmes on school days. Though the programmes were meant for children, others also viewed the programmes within the school. These were not based on school syllabi but intended to provide general enrichment. Governments of each state receiving SITE programmes were responsible for electrifying the school, which housed the television receiver.

The contents of the programmes were identified by a group of educationists drawn from NCERT. It was then placed before the senior officials of the Department of Education of each of the SIET states. ISRO produced a series of programmes in science, which aimed at developing scientific thinking. Production studio was also set up by ISRO in Bombay and its staff developed one of the educational series. Programmes were produced at three Base Production Centres: Delhi (Hindi), Cuttack (Oriya) and Hyderabad (Telgu and Kannada). The format of the programmes was lecture, demonstration followed by documentary, drama and discussion. Before approaching the programmes for broadcast purpose, a few prototypes were produced and pretested in different villages. The purpose of this pretesting was to test the acceptability of the programmes.

Experience during SITE period was quiet encouraging for further expansion of television service in the country. Government decided to start the SITE continuity community-viewing programme. Forty per cent of the villages were provided community-viewing facility in six SITE cluster areas by setting terrestrial transmitters. This was made possible because the infrastructure existed and studio facilities developed during SITE terrestrial transmission were made available from 1977 to 1982 and educational programmes were available in the morning hours along with other programmes in the evening.

An important highlight for SITE was teacher training through multimedia. Nearly 50,000 teachers were exposed to this training in two installments. Experts planned the lessons. SITE experiment drew attention of the world. Two international teams, one sponsored by the United Nations and the other by the Commonwealth Broadcasting Association toured the SITE areas and gave favourable reactions.

Kheda Communication Project (KCP)

The Kheda Communication Project (KCP) was conducted between 1975 and 1990 in Kheda district of Gujarat. In the project, a low power transmitter in the village was set up in Ahemadabad. This was linked to studio earth station. Through this, local programme and the central satellite programmes were relayed. The project covered 400 villages and 550 community sets were provided. The transmission time was for 90 minutes. Space Application Centre (SAC) and Doordarshan contributed the programmes. SAC produced mainly development and education programmes and Doordarshan contributed news, topical issues and entertainment programmes. The experiment was an innovation and a milestone in the history of Indian television.

The project was evaluated and studies indicated gains in the level of knowledge in TV villages on health such as cholera symptoms, prevention of malaria and immunization programme. Higher knowledge level was indicated in agricultural practices related to soil testing, advantages of using high yielding seeds etc. (Phutela, 2004)

Indian National Satellite (INSAT)

The SITE implemented in India in 1975-76 received great applause at national as well as international levels. This unique success with a borrowed satellite for one year encouraged India to have its own satellite. In 1977, India approved a proposal to launch a multipurpose and space communication system of her own, called Indian National Satellite (INSAT). The major objectives of INSAT were:

- To produce and transmit varied programmes designed to awaken, inform, enlighten, educate, entertain and enrich all sections of the people in different parts of the country.
- To promote alternative approaches to education for children, youth and adults.
- To stimulate interest and involvement of people in economic development.
- To stimulate interest and involvement of people in economic development.

INSAT-1A was launched and placed in its orbit on April 10, 1982. According to Indian specifications and requirements, it was designed and fabricated by Ford Aerospace and

Communications Corporation (FACC), USA. It was a joint venture of the Department of Space, Posts and Telegraphs, Meteorological Department, Ministry of Information and Broadcasting and Ministry of Education and Culture. All these government agencies used the satellite to reach the target groups. The Ministry of Education had a special commitment to use its facility for fulfilling the educational priorities.

INSAT-1A developed mechanical snags and in September 1982 it ceased to function. However, INSAT-1B was launched on August 30, 1983. INSAT project covered six of the educationally backward states as in SITE. About four thousand television sets were installed and commissioned.

These television programmes were telecast in the morning and evening. Morning transmission was devoted to school education for children in the age group of 5-8 years and 9-12 years. These programmes were not only syllabus oriented but provided broader perspectives of enriching school lessons. Local Doordarshan Kendras and Central Institute of Educational Technology, and NCERT produced the programmes. Evening television programmes were mainly developmental and national programmes and included news, films and live telecasts.

India's space programmes took another big leap on July 24, 1993 when the multi-functional indigenously built satellite INSAT-2B was blasted off into space by Arriane launch vehicle from KOUROV, French Guyana in South America. INSAT-2 satellite is a multipurpose satellite providing space services for telecommunication, meteorological observations and data relay, nation wide TV broadcasting, radio and TV distribution, disaster warning and distress alert sources. It has 50 per cent higher communication capacity than the first generation INSAT-1 satellite.

Countrywide Classroom (CWC)

In the draft of the Sixth Five-Year Plan (1980-1985), the University Grants Commission proposed the establishment of centres of mass communication and educational technology in selected universities in the country. With the launching of INSAT in April 1982, the UGC-INSAT television project, namely 'Countrywide Classroom' was launched to bring qualitative and quantitative improvements in higher education. CWC was launched on August 15, 1984.

The objectives of the broadcast were to upgrade, update and enrich the quality of education at tertiary level. The programmes sought to arouse interest of viewers, and to broaden their perspective.

The primary target audience of CWCR project are the undergraduate college students studying in colleges located in the smaller towns and rural areas. Other college students and teachers are the secondary audience but a large and interested non-student population also views these programmes. From a small number of four EMRCs and two AVRCs in 1984, CWCR programmes are now produced in eleven EMRCs and ten AVRCs. The Consortium is coordinating the programmes for Educational Communication (CEC) of UGC. UGC has provided television sets to different colleges to enable viewing by students and teachers. UGC hands over the programmes to Doordarshan for telecast. The one-hour UGC programmes are telecast through satellite all over the country in the morning on all days except Saturdays and Sundays. The programmes are produced in subject areas of languages, social sciences, engineering, technology, and sciences etc.

National Council of Educational Research and Training

NCERT is the national resource organization set up by the Government of India to assist and advice the central and state governments on academic matters related to school education. As one of its activities, NCERT conducts programmes for capacity building of teacher education institutions at the state level. NCERT conducted two major experiments using television. A brief on both the experiments is described below:

Programme of Mass Orientation of School Teachers (PMOST)

The National Policy on Education 1986 gave a significant emphasis to teachers' status and their training. Keeping this in view as well as to orient teachers on the new thrusts of the new educational policy, the Department of Education, Ministry of Human Resource Development, Government of India, prepared a centrally sponsored scheme of in-service education of primary teachers. The scheme conceptualized a massive teacher orientation programme covering about half a million teachers annually for the period 1986-90. NCERT planned the details of the programme and developed the instructional materials and the training package. The actual programme was implemented in collaboration with the SCERTs.

The objectives of the Programme of Mass Orientation of School Teachers (PMOST) were to:

1. revitalize the organizational structure for the training of teachers and other educational functionaries;
2. develop models for continuing education of teachers and other functionaries; and

3. effectively use mass media for the in-service education and training of teachers.

The in-service teacher education package was transacted through participatory and interactive approaches. Each participant had an opportunity to express his/her views in the context of each topic. The teachers participated in the discussions where the focus was on the appropriateness of teaching learning strategies in locale specific context. An 'In-service Teacher Education Package', comprising print and non-print materials formed the main basis of training. The print materials for primary and upper primary school teachers, course directors and resource persons were developed in Hindi, English and other regional languages. The non-print material included video films, audio programmes and other various activities. The modules on the teaching of subjects included modern methodologies of teaching and practical exercises on classroom teaching.

NCERT constituted a resource group with experts in different areas for the orientation of state level functionaries – the principals, teacher educators, educational supervisors and in-service education experts. The state level key persons, in turn, trained the resource persons. The resource persons, in turn, oriented batches of 50 teachers in each course. There were four cycles of teacher orientation programmes in one centre. There was also provision for guest speakers.

PMOST being a national level project, was continuously monitored and evaluated in order to increase its relevance and effectiveness. NCERT developed guidelines in 1988 for conducting follow up studies. The Regional Colleges of Education at Bhopal, Bhubaneshwar and Mysore were involved in this evaluation.

In Karnataka, the study revealed that the PMOST programme created sufficient awareness among the teacher participants though there were a number of problems. No information was provided for the third level participants when programmes were organized for II and III level trainers in day camps. The classrooms with pre-designed seating arrangements influenced the transactional methodology. The learning material was provided only on the first day, and the methodology for transaction the modules was mainly lecture-cum-discussion. The telecast programme, which was an integral component of PMOST, was not utilized due to lack of TV sets, and inconvenient timing. The study further revealed that the funds provided by NCERT were inadequate.

In Madhya Pradesh, it was found that the training camps were successful in developing awareness and knowledge of the teachers but could not develop teaching competencies for curriculum transaction. Results indicated that the instructional packages and quality of training personnel had moderate effects on the development of awareness. The objectives, such as development of values through curricular and co-curricular activities, were not achieved. Modules were not self-explanatory and training was given through lecture and discussion methods. Also the teachers did not use the telecasts. Results indicate that there was no significant increase in the competency and skill in curriculum transaction.

The Bihar study concluded that planning did not receive any attention. Resource persons were incapable of creating intellectual excitement. Participants felt that the basic facilities were not provided and Hindi versions of the modules were full of linguistic errors. Messages of the programme were lost due to the three-tier organization. Only lecture method was used in the transaction of the modules.

Evaluation done by RCE, Bhubaneshwar, revealed that there was need for coordination between various implementation agencies with regard to planning, monitoring and evaluation of various programme inputs at different levels. The content of the modules should have been restricted and should have highlighted the learning needs of various types of disadvantaged children in different subject areas. Findings revealed that average awareness had been developed among the teachers.

The PMOST covered more than five lakh (half a million) teachers within a short time. The cascade model adopted in the programme was well justified for large coverage of teachers distributed over more than 5000 blocks and a few thousand municipal wards. The cascading, however, had its toll on the quality due to steady decline in the trainer quality as one moved from national to state to the sub-state level trainers and also the usual transmission loss in all such complicated communication events.

Evaluation studies of PMOST in the experimental states concluded that the major drawback of the training programme was poor planning. There was no coordination among the implementing agencies. But the experiment created awareness among the teachers.

Special Orientation of Primary Teachers (SOPT)

Special Orientation Programme for Primary Teachers (SOPT) was another centrally sponsored scheme on in-service education of primary teachers initiated during the eighth five-year plan. NCERT was responsible for of its planning, programming, organization, conduct, monitoring and also the academic input. The Department of Teacher Education and Special Education in NCERT coordinated the programme in cooperation with national and state DPEP authorities. The scheme was launched in 1993-94 with a target of covering 4.5 lakh primary school teachers each year. SOPT was not for providing initial qualifying training to the teachers, instead it was meant for orienting teachers with a few specific schemes of the Government of India, like Minimum Levels of Learning, Operation Blackboard, etc. All States and Union Territories participated in SOPT, except Andaman and Nicobar.

The focus of SOPT was on:

- providing competencies as envisaged in the minimum levels of learning,
- developing competencies in the use of Operation Blackboard material in primary school, and
- encouraging teachers to adopt child centered approaches to learning and encourage participation of trainees with a focus on skill and activity based teaching learning processes.

The model for training was the cascade model where the master trainers at the national level provided training to key resource persons of the state nodal agencies. They were the subject experts. Key persons trained the resource persons and the resource persons, in turn, trained the primary school teachers. The training centres were selected on the basis of availability of physical infrastructure at the centres. The duration of training for key persons was five days and that for the resource persons and primary teachers, it was seven days.

The teachers were provided with self-instructional printed material, containing 16 articles. These articles addressed basic strategies and concerns incorporated in NPE (1986) and POA

(1992). The write-ups were on Operation Blackboard Scheme, Minimum Levels of Learning, Continuous Evaluation, Developing School Readiness in Children, creating school climate for effective teaching learning, education of special groups, girls education and value education. Training materials on curricular areas related to teaching of mother tongue, teaching of mathematics, teaching of environment studies, social studies and science, art education, work experience at primary level and health and physical education.

The style of presentation of reading material was interactive and incorporated a number of activities and built-in evaluation exercises. The idea of training for one week was that a teacher will be in a position to develop confidence. For the key persons, and the resource persons, NCERT developed a training manual. This manual provided explanatory notes for each training session. It also provided guidelines regarding planning, organization and management of training. Along with the printed material, video films, audio cassettes and users' guide were also developed. During the training, Operation Blackboard (OB) kits were used which were provided to the primary schools. These OB kits were used to teach concepts. The monitoring visits and guidance to the faculty and trainees were carried out by a team of experts from the Elementary Education Bureau (which also looks after teacher education) of Ministry of Human Resource Development. The actual in-service education programmes were conducted by the DIETs and other institutes identified by the State Government or the SCERTs. The NCERT provided the funds to the states with predetermined expenditure norms. However, states were free to augment the SOPT funds with their own resources. For example, Andhra Pradesh provided per diem at its own state norms, which was higher than the norm prescribed by NCERT for SOPT; the difference was paid for by the state government simultaneously extending the programme by two additional days to the prescribed norm of SOPT. The total allocation to SOPT was Rs 40 crores or about US $13 million.

While SOPT was implemented through cascading, two specific experiments were made using distance education modality. For training of primary school teachers under SOPT in Karnataka, about 1000 teachers were called to the training centres established by the Department of Personnel and Administration; the centres were equipped with dish antenna for receiving signals through Training and Development Communication Channel (TDCC). The lessons were delivered by expert trainers in Kannada from the studio of Indira Gandhi National Open University in New Delhi uplinked through the earth station parked in its Maidan Garhi Campus. The trainees asked questions and comments were given through telephone and fax. With the encouraging results of the first experiment, this approach was repeated in July 1996 for training of more than 1500 primary school teachers in Madhya Pradesh. The tutors/trainers received a large number of questions every day.

Indira Gandhi National Open University (IGNOU)

IGNOU, established by an Act of Parliament in 1985, has an objective to take education to the doorsteps of the students and provide education to all, irrespective of age, region or formal qualification. It also offers need based vocational and professional academic programmes. The university has a nationwide network of study centres, which are equipped with tape recorders, VCRs, Color TV sets, audio and videocassettes, besides print materials. IGNOU has a full-fledged communication division – Electronic Media and

Production Centre, which produces audio and video programmes and organizes educational broadcasts over television and radio for the benefit of students as well as the general public.

Broadcast of IGNOU's educational programmes began in May 1991 on the national network of Doordarshan thrice a week in the early morning. The broadcasts of audio programmes began in January 1992 from Bombay and Hyderabad and later from Delhi and Lucknow. The IGNOU programmes are syllabus based and cater to the learners enrolled in IGNOU programmes. These programmes supplement the self-instructional texts provided to the students of the university. These broadcasts mark a major step in the progress of IGNOU in fulfilling its educational objectives and in the country's development.

Gyan Darshan

Gyan Darshan (GD) is an exclusive and dedicated twenty-four hour educational and developmental TV channel of India. It is a joint collaborative venture of Ministry of Human Resource Development (MHRD), Information & Broadcasting Ministry, IGNOU, UGC, CEC, NCERT, CIET, SIETs, National Institute of Open Schooling (NIOS), Department of Space and Technology, IITs, Technical Teachers Training Institute's, Department of Space, DECU, Ministries of Rural Development, Health, Labour, Environment, National Aids Control Organisation (NACO) etc. It was inaugurated on 26 January, 2000. EMPC of IGNOU has been identified as the coordinating and transmission agency.

Gyan Darshan telecasts educational programmes from school level to tertiary level through different cable operators in the country for wider outreach. It offers interesting and informative programmes of relevance and value to specialized categories – pre-school kids, primary and secondary school children, college/university students, youth seeking career opportunities, housewives, adults and many others. This channel is accessible to an estimated 28 million viewers in 40 lakh cable homes spread all over India. The technical arrangement for Gyan Darshan is that the earth station has been set up with a 7.2 m antenna with arrangements for the play of pre-taped programmes from the Earth Room Station itself while others can be viewed from Video Studio-II. Microwave links to enable live relay of the channel from EMPC to Doordarshan Kendra, Delhi, and to source programme from the CIET studios have been installed. The footprint of the satellite is the entire country and GD signals can be conveniently received without any special equipment anywhere. Gyan Darshan as it entered in its fourth year on January 26, 2004, went completely digital. It has expanded into a bouquet of channels namely GD-1, GD-2, GD-3 Eklavya and GD-4 Vyas.

GD-1 is a twenty-four hour channel devoted to education and distance education. The transmission for curriculum based and enrichment programmes are each of 12 hour duration. The programmes of IGNOU and CIET-NCERT, including NIOS, are telecast for four hours each, IIT programmes for three hours, CEC-UGC programmes for two and half-hours and one hour each for TTTI and adult education.

GD-2 is devoted entirely to interactive distance education. It is a one way video and two ways audio satellite based interactive system operating on the C-Band transponder of INSAT-3C. (Details of interactive experiments are discussed in Chapter Four).

The third channel GD-3 Eklavya, is the technology channel which brings quality education to the students pursuing engineering education throughout the country. Eklavya features lectures of the courses taught at the IITs situated at Kharagpur, Mumbai, Kanpur, Delhi, Guwahati, Roorkee and Chennai. Eklavya transmits 24 hours daily, with eight courses running in parallel. These are repeated once for the benefit of those who may have missed viewing the first time. This pattern continues from Monday to Saturday. Sundays are reserved for special interest programmes on Technology and Science *(EMPC IGNOU, June 2005)*. Eklavya – Technology channel reaches every corner of the country through INSAT-3C Satellite on C-Band (74 degrees East), Downlink frequency 4165 MHz.

Another channel in the bouquet of Gyan Darshan is GD-4 Vyas which brings quality education to the students pursuing higher education throughout the country. Higher education in India has expanded significantly. Every district and small town of the country has colleges providing higher education to people. Today those enrolled for higher education account for 9 million students in nearly 13,000 colleges and 234 institutions of higher education.

The aim of this channel is to bridge the knowledge and information gap in the area of higher education and provide information to all those who need it. The Vision 2020 envisages India to be a knowledge super power. Higher education has to play a key role. Universities and colleges provide higher education to nearly nine million students. The vision of Vyas therefore, is to reach out to large number of students, teachers and general public with quality educational material electronically so as to address the issues of access and equity with quality higher education.

The Missions of this channel are:

- To find out knowledge need of the people through research and address the same by developing "knowledge resources" with the help and support of research facilities available in the universities and colleges of the country.
- To bridge this gap by making quality knowledge packages delivered by the best teachers available and those too to everyone who desires to benefit from it.

Vyas will function in a manner that a student could register for a certificate, diploma or a degree level programme. It would be so organized that it maintains the sequencing of the lessons and the repetition schedules. In this effort, the 24-hour channel would enter into specific arrangements with several mix-mode learning programmes currently being offered by many Indian universities.

This channel chooses such subjects as are in high demand but lack adequate number of competent teachers. It also selects such subjects which are difficult to be explained optimally by conventional classroom tools but could be effectively covered in the visual multi-media animated form for competitive examinations, women and general public.

The primary target audiences of the channel are the students studying in undergraduate and postgraduate classes in universities and colleges all over the country, particularly in small towns. Students pursuing correspondence courses, teachers teaching undergraduate and postgraduate courses and also the staff of training colleges, and students appearing for various competitive examinations watch this channel. The channel acts as a tool for the audience to take up fresh initiative in broadening their horizon especially in the field of career enhancement. The Vyas programmes are telecast round the clock on GD-4 and some are relayed on GD-1.

Conclusion

Educational Radio Broadcast began in 1930s and Educational Television in 60s. Educational broadcasting in India has a long and rich history. It has crossed many important milestones. It is probably the only national system that has learnt to offer educational programmes in more than 16 languages. The mainframe broadcasting has been resilient with the development of technology adapting to digital technology and interactive media. There are, however, several mileposts yet to be covered.

The enthusiasm in educational broadcasting is yet to be matched with its acceptability in the community of teachers and students and form the central core of the educational system. Broadcast radio and educational television programmes in education are only marginally used. There is little evidence that educational broadcast programmes have impact on student learning. There is no significant place for development of skills and competence in use of educational media as the central process of instruction. In the scheme of teacher education, it is taught as theoretical subject that too in very few universities.

A closer look at the ethos of culture of education indicates that educational media is still seen only as an 'isle' on the wall, and not as part of the system. Just as technology is not part of the social culture, educational technology – media and broadcasting – are yet to become a part of the culture of education. The future challenge of educational broadcasting is to become more relevant, relating directly to the stakes of the learners, and be subsumed as the cultural ethos of education in general and educational institutions in particular.

4

Interactive Television

Introduction

In this chapter we will only restrict ourselves to interactive television experiments conducted by various organizations in India.

Interactive Television is emerging as a new media and tool for conferencing, training and education. Interactive Television (ITV) is a television with interactive content. It refers to two way electronic communication between two or more groups or three or more individuals who are in separate locations. It combines traditional TV watching with interactivity of the Internet and personal computer. This two-way electronic communication is also known as Teleconferencing. It is divided into three major types: audio, video and computer.

Audio Teleconferencing: Audio Teleconferencing is actually telephone conferencing. In this, the speakerphones are available in the classrooms. This system can be used for upto ten participants. If there are more people, more sophisticated speakers can be used which are available. Audio conferencing is used because telephones are available all over the world. Also conferences can be arranged at a short notice. Compared to other technologies, the cost is low. There are different types of audio conferencing like: Dedicated Conference Networks; Dial Up Networks; Meet Me Conferencing and Direct Dial Conferencing Systems. There is another type of audio conferencing known as Audio Graphic. Audio Graphic is the transmission of print and graphic information through telephone lines.

Video Teleconferencing: This is a combination of audio and visual media which provides interactive voice communication and television pictures. This system comprises one-way or two-way video and two-way audio networks. Motion video is the most common technology but other options also exist, such as freeze-frame television, compressed video systems and full motion video systems. Video conferencing is a national conferencing format but involves high cost.

Computer Conferencing: In this system two or more people communicate with each other via computer terminal. Here, participants can write their message into the computer, which can be retrieved and answered later.

ITV is being used by many educational institutions and corporations for Tele-Training and group meetings. It provides richer entertainment and more information. In education, ITV is useful as it:

- provides expert instructors to remote schools, colleges, universities and offices;
- offers uniform, quality instruction to learners scattered over many sites or over a large area;
- allows learners at multiple locations to interact with the expert and with each other; and
- provides in-service training without leaving the workplace.

ITV requires three components: The Satellite Transponder; the Hub and a studio uplinked with earth station that can uplink the programme to the satellite and reception centres with direct reception facilities which can download the programmes uplinked from the studio at the Hub.

The above three components are further supported by telephone, STD and computer network. The hub, the satellite and reception centres are used for transmission from the teaching end to the learning end. The telephone, fax, computer communication, particularly e-mail, is used for communication from the learning end to the reception end.

Training and Development Communication Channel (TDCC)

Government of India, particularly the Department of Space, allocated the spare life of earlier generation satellite for experimentation in human resources development. It is called Training and Development Communication Channel (TDCC). The Training and Development Communication Channel provides one-way video and two-way audio teleconferencing network for the interactive training and education. The TDCC on INSAT is operational since February 1995. Since its inception, the TDCC is being utilized considerably. The activities are being expanded to cover new users, areas and applications. The aim of TDCC is for training and development communication in the country. TDCC is not a channel for one-way broadcasting, it is for interactive training and education. The advantages of this system are (ISRO 2000):

1. Training simultaneously in the shortest time to a large number of people who are geographically dispersed,
2. Multiplier effects by training of trainers,
3. Uniformity of the training content,
4. Access to the best available learning resources, irrespective of geographical locations of the learners,

5. Repeatability of training courses/educational packages, easy updating and dissemination,
6. Enhanced involvement of the trainers/learners due to interaction capability and therefore, greater learning gains,
7. Capability to share the same network by different user groups. Specific topics for specific locations and for specific groups are also possible,
8. Significant savings in expenditure due to economics in travel, logistics and replication of teaching infrastructure, and
9. Can effectively supplement the conventional system of training and in some cases can itself become the major component of the training system.

TDCC system earlier consisted of one extended C-band transponder (Channel-15) of INSAT-2C and two teaching end facilities (studio and uplink), one at IGNOU campus, New Delhi (using Transportable Remote Area Communication Tract (TRACT) of SAC, and TV studio of IGNOU. The other is at SAC Campus, Ahmedabad [using Ahmedabad Earth Station (AES) of SAC and TV studio of DECU]. Also the Satellite News Gathering Terminal (SNGT) of ISRO is temporarily located in Madhya Pradesh Academy of Administration, Bhopal. DECU acts as a nodal agency for TDCC with SAC providing the uplink and technology inputs (ISRO 2000).

The TDCC system network consists of teaching end, the spacecraft and the classroom. The teaching end consists of a small studio and an uplink earth station. From this studio, live lectures or recorded video programmes are telecasts. The television signals are uplinked to a geostationary communication satellite by an uplink earth station that is located at the teaching end. In the TDCC network-4 C-Band transponders are earmarked. The classroom has the Direct Reception System terminal, which has the capacity of receiving a signal in C-band from the satellite. The talkback is possible through normal STD telephone or fax provided in the classrooms. The questions from the classroom are received at the studios and heard live over the network by all. The resource persons sitting in the studio provide the answers.

There are a number of organizations in the country who use regularly the TDCC channel. These are Open and Distance Education Institutions like IGNOU, and national institutions like NCERT, NIEPA and NIOS. The other agencies are state government departments (agriculture, forestry, watershed management, women and child development and panchyati raj) and private organizations. Majority of the users use it for training and capacity building.

Experiments for Rural Development

- Satellite based teleconferencing for training and development by Remote Sensing and Communication, Gandhinagar: RESECO was started in 1995 with the help of ISRO. Government of Gujarat has set up its own teaching end, comprising studio and uplinking facilities at RESECO. The receiving facilities are at 150 locations and sets are being set up at the block level. The state government has its own network with return audio and video through web camera that is used for governance and administrative purposes.
- Satellite Communication for Rural Development by Abdul Nazir Sahib-State Institute of Rural Development (ANS-SIRD) SATCOM Centre, Mysore: This project started in

> 1995 using ISRO facilities at Bangalore. The state departments, like rural development, agriculture, education and health, took the initiative in setting up their own studio and uplinking facilities at AMS-SIRD SATCOM centre at Mysore in 2001. The project covers all the 20 districts of the state. Receiving sets have been provided at DIETs. Facilities at the Block level are to be expanded by installing 259 additional DRS TV sets.
>
> *Source*: Trivedi (2005).

Indira Gandhi National Open University

IGNOU is the first university, which started the ITV in India for educational purposes. Interactive Television is part of IGNOUs instructional system. It gives the learners who are at far ends a direct access to the experts who are at the studios. The satellite based one-way video and two-way audio teleconferencing was first conducted in 1993 in collaboration with the ISRO on experimental basis. The target audiences were the Regional Directors, Assistant Regional Directors and Academic Counsellors posted at different regional centres. This experiment was successful and since then Interactive sessions are regularly held by various schools of IGNOU for distance teaching. These sessions are conducted by School of Management (CEMBA/CEMPA Programmes), School of Social Sciences, School of Education, School of Health Sciences, School of Continuing Education etc. Teleconference sessions are also conducted for orientation of academic counselors of management and commerce disciplines. In the certificate programme on "Empowering Women Through Self Help Groups", women interact directly with the experts through teleconference sessions. The women empowerment project has established

150 programme centres all over the country with the DRS. School of Education conducts teleconference sessions in their Post Graduate Diploma in Higher Education (PGDHE) programme. PGDHE programme was launched by IGNOU in 1992 for teachers who aspire to teach in universities and colleges. The programme comprises five courses and a project. One of the course is the Extended Contact Programme (ECP). The ECP is partly organized through teleconference mode. IGNOU has experimented the ECP through teleconferencing in 1993. The faculty of School of Education and other outside experts conduct discussion and have video presentations. The teleconferencing assigns an activity that a learner is supposed to undertake following the session. At the end of the session, which is approximately of one hour, 30-35 minutes are devoted for interaction where all the learners and resource persons take part in the ECP linked through the teleconferencing network. Learners ask questions, raise issues, share experiences and apprehensions.

Of late teleconference sessions are being conducted by the Vice Chancellor for meeting with the Regional Directors/ Assistant Regional Directors to exchange information and review performance. Induction programmes for new students are also conducted through teleconference. In the year 2003-2004, 429 hours of teleconferencing was conducted. Of this 273 hrs were for internal use pertaining to IGNOU programmes and 156 hrs for external use (IGNOU Profile 2004). Teleconferencing in IGNOU are being regularly held for tele-counselling, tele-collaboration, tele-teaching, educational seminars etc. Gyan Darshan Channel-2 is entirely devoted to interactive distance education. IGNOU has provided the facility for interaction from various parts of the country with the studio with a toll free number.

IGNOU-AIR Interactive Radio Counselling

- In May 1998, the IGNOU-AIR interactive radio counselling was started for students of open/conventional universities. IGNOU collaborated with AIR Bhopal and started the project. The experiment was successful and therefore extended to other AIR stations. The focus of the counselling sessions is the academic subjects. At present, these sessions are broadcast from 189 AIR stations in India. IGNOU is using this mode to reach the isolated and remote areas. On the first and the third Sundays of every month, IRC is on National Broadcast Network. The session is for one hour. Similarly, on the second and fourth (fifth) Sundays of every month, the session is of one hour in all the AIR stations, except Srinagar where pre-recorded lessons are broadcast at night for one hour. The state open universities conduct the IRCs from Ahmedabad, Bhopal, Bangalore, Patna, Jaipur, Kolkata, Hyderabad and Mumbai on the fourth Sunday of every month.
- A few evaluation studies on interactive radio counselling have been reported. *Chaudhary and Bansal* (2000), *Sukumar* (2001) and *Sharma* (2002) found that the participants appreciated the interactive radio counseling sessions. However, it was found that there was need to encourage interactivity amongst the listeners. Non-students also make use of these programmes. Learners suggested the use of local language for interaction.

Source: EMPC IGNOU, June 2005.

National Institute of Educational Planning and Administration (NIEPA)

NIEPA is an apex institution in the field of educational planning and administration. Its prime concern is capacity building in educational policy, planning and management through research, training, consultancy and dissemination. NIEPA conducts many interactive television experiments. It has conducted a number of training programmes for the principals of DIETs. Most of the NIEPAs interactive programmes are experimented with behavioural science sessions which normally are built around simulations, games, survey feedback technique, role play, case studies and the like. In one of the programmes, the participants were taught SWOT analysis. Experts analysed the SWOT on the television. It was a replica for a classroom where survey feedback and simulations were used. In another programme an outside experts presentation was recorded on a video. The video was played and participants all over the centres were encouraged to ask questions.

> One of the major experiments conducted through this mode by NIEPA was in July 1997. The experiment was a prelude to the world conference on "Education India – The Next Millennium". There were two important dimensions of this experiment – the content and the virtuality of the conference. The one-day experiment was divided into four sessions. The first theme was Education for All, the second on Education and the World of Work. The focus of this session was on higher education. The third theme focussed on Educational Financing. The last session was on Quality of Education. The conference was participated by over 125 persons at different locations of the country. Among the participants were education secretaries, former vice chancellors, directors, professors and members of different NGOs.

Classroom 2000 +

Classroom 2000 + was a technology demonstration project sponsored by Indo-US Sub-commission and implemented by Central Institute of Educational Technology, NCERT, New

Delhi. The project was executed in collaboration with the Doordarshan, the Computer Maintenance Corporation (CMC) and Kendriya Vidyalaya Sangathan. Some of the hardware, computer software and technical guidance were provided by Kentucky Educational Television Network, USA.

The experiment was carried out in five Kendriya Vidyalays – one each in Bombay, Calcutta, Madras, Hyderabad, Ghaziabad and Navyug School, Delhi. Students were from Class XII. A class of five students was also set up at CIET, NCERT. In each city one more Kendriya Vidyalay was chosen to act as a control group. The TV lessons were, however, available on the national network and the regional networks and were viewed in schools and homes.

The demonstration lessons were given for 5 days, May 3-7, 1993, in the morning from 9 to 12 noon. Everyday there was one lesson of 45 minutes in Maths and Physics. There were three themes in Mathematics and two themes in Physics. The classrooms of the participation schools were equipped with a color TV monitor, keypads, computer and a telephone. Telephone and computerized response system established the communication between the participating students and the TV teacher in the CIET studio. The computerized response system in each school consisted of a keypad for each participating student, a classroom computer and two STD telephone lines. Out of these two, one line was used for data transmission and the other for voice communication. The TV teacher asked multiple-choice questions flashed on TV screen. The students entered their responses into the keypad. The answers were responded, the graph was made and the correct answer given by the TV teacher. Students could check their responses with the answer given by the TV teacher. Students posed questions and sought clarifications from the teacher/experts through STD lines. Even the name and photograph of the student asking question was flashed on the TV screen.

The live TV lessons from the TV studios in CIET were sent to Doordarshan via microwave link and then uplinked to satellite for transmission. The existing facilities in the studio were augmented for the purpose of live transmission. There were four cameras, including the camera installed for getting the written word by the TV teacher and the expert presenting the lesson. Subject teachers in Physics and Mathematics were available in CIET on telephone lines to manage incoming calls.

Indian Institute of Technology

The interactive teleconferencing course on "Innovations in Teaching Methodology for Higher Order Learning" was conducted by the Indian Institute of Technology, Delhi. The experiment was held in March 1996 from the IGNOU studio by employing ISRO uplink and transponder facilities. It was a unique experiment on satellite, telecommunication mode of offering live and interactive courses for distant learners. The objectives of the course were to:

- explain higher order learning processes,
- describe logical process for innovation,
- plan instruction by objectives,
- employ group dynamics and interactivity,
- select and employ audio visuals,
- design innovative laboratory experiments,
- list elements of quality in education, and
- assess higher order learning.

The course was for the faculty members teaching AICTE

approved degree level engineering institutions. The participants were from Ahmedabad, Bangalore, Bhopal, Hyderabad, Jaipur, Madras and Delhi. The studio was transformed into a classroom with a chalkboard, OHP and a dais for the resource persons. Other hardware resources like computer and computer projection system, slide projector, VCR and monitors were also kept for the resource persons. This was done with the intention that the faculty participants identify it as a classroom type teaching.

The main focus of the course was on the ways and means of creating higher order learning of students. The course was confined to methodologies of higher order learning in science and engineering at the university level from where the target participants were taken. Higher Order Learning was conceptualized as learning with greater mental processing and discovery learning as against non-higher order learning. It is concerned with the higher levels of taxonomy in the Bloom's domains of learning.

The course was for one week. It was planned as a participatory and informal face-to-face contact course with ingredients of assignments and hands-on experience. The concept and technique of microteaching for self-improvement of faculty members was also introduced. A local participant did it by introducing and by conducting a multi skill micro teaching session. Participants viewed the session live and filled up their graphical rating scales which were made available to them by post.

Assignments were given in two different sessions. These were to plan and prepare an innovative overhead transparency; to chalk out a storyboard for a set of slides and to prepare a one-page innovative laboratory experiment sheet. These assignments were faxed by the participants to IGNOU studio or IIT campus. The assignments were reviewed and discussed on-line. Many sheets on OHP transparencies were photocopied on transparencies and the same were projected live during discussion.

The special feature of the course was the online test of the participants on the last day. Tests were projected on an overhead transparency. It was also read out for the sake of clarity. Participants were asked to stop writing, to collect their response sheets and to redistribute the same at random, one to each participant, ensuring that no one got his/her own sheet. Then all the participants were asked to assume the role of examiner and to mark the sheets with them in cooperation with the course coordinator. The coordinator projected sample acceptable responses. The alternative responses were also indicated by interaction with the local participants. The centres were requested to prepare one page mark sheets and fax the same or read it on STD phone immediately to Delhi. The entire process of conducting the on-line test just took 40 minutes. It also demonstrated the faculty participants how to conduct a class test, do marking and also provide immediate feedback and reinforcement.

There were some problems, which interrupted the transmission and communication in the course. These were video quality, power failures, voltage spikes etc.

To see the effectiveness of the course and relative gains of the participants in terms of their learning outcomes, a pretest was conducted before the commencement of the course. Pretest sheets were faxed to Delhi and same were evaluated. The online post-test to determine their exit profile was conducted in the concluding session of the course with questions of the same order of difficulty as the pretest. It showed that the post-test score was 76.4 per cent as against the pretest score of 17.5 per cent. The reactions of the participants to the academic and practical content of the course were positive. There were no dropouts in the course from any regional centre.

> The Kanwal Rekhi School of Information Technology (KresIT) at The Indian Institute of Technology, Bombay, has started the Distance Education Programme from 2002. The objective of the programme is to make lectures by the expert faculty accessible to students at far places through setting up of remote centers across the country. The lectures are broadcast using VSAT network and hence provide live interaction between the students and the faculty, There is a steady increase in the number of students and in the number of remote centres since the distance education programmes started. With the success of the programme, the faculty believes that this is the way to the future to provide quality education.
>
> *Source*: Arya, Krithivasan and Iyer, (2005).

ISRO-UGC National Talkback Experiment

A National Talkback experiment was conducted in November 1991 to study the feasibility of two-way communication in Country Wide Classroom Programme. Various agencies like UGC, DECU, ISRO, AVRCs, EMRCs and Doordarshan, collaborated in this programme. Under this experiment twelve CWCR programmes were selected for telecast. The pre-recorded programmes were beamed from the earth station to the INSAT-1D satellite. These programmes were received by students at Ahmedabad, Calcutta, Hyderabad, Imphal, Jodhpur, Madurai, Roorkee and Patiala. Two centres – Jodhpur and Imphal were linked with the studios at Delhi through satellite, whereas the other six stations were linked through PSTN. The talkback from the centres was facilitated through straight trunk dial (STD) facility of the telephone. The students put the questions to the experts at the studios. To facilitate the talkback experiment, one bilingual moderator was available at each media centre. The role of the facilitator was to establish the link between the resource person and the students. Questions were moderated and translated if required. The resource persons responded to the questions.

Distance Education Programme – Sarva Shiksha Abhiyan

Government of India launched the District Primary Education Programme (DPEP) for Primary Education Development in 1994. The DPEP programme was based on the varied experiences gained in the implementation of earlier schemes like, Andhra Pradesh Education Project, Bihar Education Project, Uttar Pradesh Basic Education Project and Lok Jumbish.

DPEP seeks to achieve UEE through district specific participative planning and management. It was implemented in a mission mode through registered state level autonomous societies to reduce gender differences in enrollment, and dropout rates to less than 10 per cent and to raise average achievement levels by at least 25 percent, over measured baseline levels. The components of the programme included construction of classrooms and new schools, opening of non formal/alternative schooling centres, training of teachers, setting up resource centres, development of teaching learning material, research based interventions, etc. In 1996, experts felt that distance education inputs and materials would facilitate the training of teachers and other personnel in primary education sector. It was decided that IGNOU should lead the project. Hence, a project proposal was developed and submitted to Ministry of Human Resource Development, Government of India, for training of primary education personnel through distance mode. The project was collaborated with NCERT and was financed by MHRD, through a loan from the International Development Association (World Bank). The aim of DPEP was to strengthen the ongoing training programmes of primary education personnel by using distance learning inputs and materials. Few areas identified in DPEP were: Development of Teaching Learning Material; Community Mobilization; Capacity Building; Strengthening of Institutions; Organizing Teleconferencing; Establishing Database etc.

In the year 1998, the scheme of Sarva Shiksha Abhiyan was evolved. The Government approved it in 2000. SSA subsumed the existing programmes like DPEP to attain universal elementary education. One of the focus of SSA is to monitor the implementation of SSA through teleconferencing and use Edusat facilities for elementary and teacher education. Thus, teleconferencing is being extensively used as a powerful mode in the DPEP – SSA project.

To conduct smooth teleconference sessions, all infrastructure facilities are checked at the teaching end, and the receiving end by DEP-SSA, New Delhi. Further, to get the desired input of teleconferencing sessions, all facilitators, observers and panelists are briefed before hand. These people are trained about the technical aspect, objective of the programme, difficulties faced during the teleconferencing session's etc. Programme schedules are prepared in advance and sent to various agencies like the studio, learning centres, the tract systems (ISRO) and the local earth stations and the panelists. Information is also obtained about the participants for building up participants profile, or recording daily feedback and formal feedback through questionnaires.

DEP provided necessary DRS for down linking facilities. In all 190 DRS were installed in DEP-DPEP districts and states and another 107 DRS has been installed under DEP-SSA at DIETs, SCERTs, SIEMATs and SPOs *(Brochure DEP-SSA)*. DEP uses one-way video and two-way audio system for teleconferences. A few teleconference sessions are provided at the national level and others are state specific programmes. From July 2003 to March 2005, four national level programmes were organised. About 2570 personnel were trained during this period. At the state level, during the same period, 62 programmes were conducted and about 22,000 personnel were trained. Teleconference sessions are organized in states of Andhra Pradesh, Assam, Chhattisgarh, Gujarat, Haryana, Himachal Pradesh, Jharkhand, Karnataka, Kerala, Madhya Pradesh, Maharashtra, Orissa, Rajasthan, Tamil Nadu, Uttaranchal, and Uttar Pradesh.

The DEP-SSA has identified the themes of the teleconferencing sessions which depends on the needs of the clientele and the state project office, administration, teachers, teacher educators etc. Reading material is developed for each theme and the target group. The material is provided at the learning center in advance so that it is used by the participants. The themes are classified into four broad categories (IGNOU-NCERT 2003):

- Building awareness,
- Contextual issues,
- Curriculum areas, and
- State-specific needs.

Under each theme there are certain programmes which are listed below:

Building Awareness	*Contextual Issues*	*Curriculum Issues*	*State Specific Needs*
• Key issues in DEP-SSA • Alternative schooling systems • Planning related to teacher training • Monitoring and Supervision • Training of VECs • Academic support to CRCs	• Education Guarantee Scheme • Integrated education for the disabled • Role and functions of VEDs, PTAs and MTAs • Gender issues • Orientation of resource Centre Coordinators	• Teacher training about environmental science at the primary stage. • Activity-based teaching of sciences • Basic concepts in mathematics at the primary stage. • Teacher training programme for languages.	• Chinnara Angla. • Kela-Kali.
• Norms related issues of DEP • Strengthening of BRCs • Monitoring of information system • Conducting of children census • Community mobilization	• Continuous comprehensive evaluation • Action research • Quality issues and strategies in primary education • Radio project • Orientation of state functionaries to Sarva Shikhsa	• Teacher training programme for English at primary stage. • Multi-level activities. • Learning theories New pedagogy. • New language project • Uses of flash cards for teaching English at primary stage.	

(*Contd.*)

(*Contd.*)

Building Awareness	*Contextual Issues*	*Curriculum Issues*	*State Specific Needs*
	• Universalisation of elementary education • Community mobilization literacy campaign	• Development of TLM (Teaching Learning Material). • Teaching science: processes. • Science curriculum (Two year B.Ed. Programme) • Pedagogical improvement in the classroom. • Project work. • Developing writing skills. Thematic integration of subjects. • Teaching mathematics (Place Value, Zero, Units, Measurements and Percentage)	

National Institute of Open Schooling

The National Institute of Open Schooling is an autonomous organization of Department of Education, Government of India. It has conducted a number of teleconference experiments. These teleconference experiments are satellite based and use one-way video and two-way audio system.

One such experiment was to orient the teachers of Gujarat, who were associated with the activities of Open Schooling. The teaching end was ISRO/DECU studio at Ahmedabad while the classrooms were at various district headquarters. The presentations were transmitted to the satellite through the ISRO studio. 300 teachers participated in this programme. The programme was of three days duration and included the following areas:

- Concept of Open Schooling
- Role of Teacher in a Study Center
- Interactive Instruction
- Counselling: Need and Relevance
- Tutor Marked Assessment
- Examination and Clarification

The evaluation of the programme revealed that teleconference was a potential instructional tool for enriching education and professional training.

Another programme which was an orientation programme for the newly enrolled students of Delhi Region was organized in 1998. The orientation covered:

- Concept and features of open schooling
- Process of learning and learning habits

- Features of self instructional material
- Purpose of PCP and preparation for examination

Another teleconference programme was organized for newly inducted coordinators. The coordinators were oriented in various aspects of open learning and management of support services in the study centres.

Jhabua Development Communication Project

Jhabua Development Communication Project (JDCP) was based on satellite communication system dedicated to meet the requirements of rural areas. DECU was the main implementing agency with technical support provided by Space Applications Centre (SAC), Ahmedabad. Others involved in the project were the tribal people of Jhabua district plus an institutional arrangement involving a large number of state government departments, Central government ministries, many non-government organizations and the entire district and state government administration. The beneficiaries of this project were – the children, women and men of Jhabua and through them the rest of the country.

The project had two main components: the broadcasting and the interactive component. It provided a communication support to the development of Jhabua in a systematic way in terms of both hardware and contents and approach of the television programmes. The first phase had the main elements of system configuration, which included installation of Direct Reception System (DRS) in carefully selected 150 villages, 12 talkback terminals at block headquarters and a studio and earth station at ISRO campus Ahmedabad. Sets were installed in community buildings accessible to majority of the people. The project acts on two fronts. For the target audience it broadcasts development oriented programmes every evening. Simultaneously it conducts training programmes in the afternoon for village functionaries and village level participants. The hallmark of TV programmes is an innovative imaginative software approach using sophisticated modern tools and yet rooted in the cultural ethos of the tribal people. These programmes are entertaining, enjoyable and educational. The programmes were made with the active participation of the local population.

Looking at the successful implementation of JDCP, the Government of India sanctioned the expansion of the project to cover the tribal areas of neighboring districts. 200 villages each in Dhar and Badwani districts were identified. In addition seven blocks in each of these two districts had talkback facilities. Apart from this the Jhabua district had an expanded coverage by providing DRS at all the Gram Panchayats.

Since the start of the programmes in 1996, two hours of development-oriented programmes are transmitted every evening and regular interactive training programmes are organized for field staff and rural audiences. Programmes or development topics were produced in-house as well as by a panel of private producers. Substantial social research is undertaken to support programme production feedback and evaluation of both interactive and broadcast programmes.

The expansion of JDCP should lead to similar projects in other parts of the country contributing to strengthening of rural development communication system. The operations will be handed over to Madhya Pradesh Government. JDCP evening transmission will soon be scheduled from Bhopal. The important objective of the Jhabua project is to contribute to the evolution of the Gramsat concept and hand it over to the State Government.

National Informatics Centre

National Informatics Centre provides videoconferencing services from 206 cities in India since 1995 including all north eastern state capitals over its high-speed satellite based network called NICNET. All the locations are connected in a star configuration. This satellite-based communication delivers high-speed data and provides videoconferencing at remote locations. NIC has invested in an in-house Multipoint Conference Server (MCS). MCS enables different networks, bandwidths and types of endpoints to communicate effectively. Through MCS, 8 sites can conference with each other at a time. It has a feature of selecting one site on a full screen and then rejoining CP mode. NIC supports international connectivity using public ISDN facility. The networks used for NIC's videoconferencing are: two SCPC VSATs and SCPC DAMA Network Management System at New Delhi. Various ministries and central and state departments are using the NIC videoconferencing services. It also supports public and private organizations.

Goa University

Goa University uses an innovative approach to upgrade knowledge base via distance education to improve the quality of education in Goa. It is an interactive mode supported by ISRO. Goa University has a studio from where lectures are broadcast by the experts. There are about 100 receiving centres and the system caters to colleges, and polytechnics. The experts are not only heard but seen. This idea was mooted by the Vice Chancellor of Goa University, Prof. B.S. Sonde.

Indian Institute of Management

The IIM, Kozhikode, launched the interactive distance education programme-using the satellite based infrastructure. It delivers real time live education to all participants by high quality video/audio and data delivered over multi-media mode. Specific management courses are simultaneously transmitted to several centres in India from a classroom in Calicut, with the help of telecommunication and satellite television transmission.

Telemedicine

Telemedicine is a recent application of the satellite communication. Through this the medical facility can be available to the remote areas of the country. The expert consultancy obtained for the patients in the remote areas from specialist in speciality hospitals have been set up for telemedicine in Bangalore, Kolkata and Tripura. ISRO has provided its SPACENET territory private hospital at Chennai and a rural hospital at Argonda in Andhra Pradesh.

All India Management Association

The All India Management Association (AIMA) – Center for Management Education (CME), New Delhi launched a project known as 'Management Education Through Technological Advancement' (META) referred to as Satellite Instructional Network (SINET) for distance education in management to working persons.

The broad objectives of the SINET were as follows:

- To provide effective satellite based interactive (one-way video, two-way audio) network system as an instrument of providing distance education in an open education delivery system.

- To provide insight into the organizational, managerial and technical subjects which form part of curriculum of various AIMA-CME programmes.
- To provide feedback mechanism for making the system more responsive in distance education, training and management.

SINET experiment in distance education involved Development and Educational Communication Unit (DECU), Indian Space Research Organization (ISRO). AIMA-CME, had the responsibility of providing all the pedagogic inputs in terms of faculty, infrastructure support at various local receiving centres and programme coordination. The students who participated in SINET were working graduates, doing management course.

There were 12 local resource centres, apart from one in New Delhi. INSAT-2A extended C-band was exclusively devoted and utilized for telecast.

In SINET VII and VIII, essentially classroom conventional teaching approach was followed. Out of four days programme in each SINET, half a day was devoted to a teleseminar sponsored by a company.

In SINET VII, actual teleteaching was carried out for three days totaling fifteen hours. The telelectures were of 30, 45, 60 and 75 minutes duration including question answer session.

Both telephone and fax facilities were available to the students for asking questions. In both SINET programmes, question-answer session formed an integral part of teleteaching. Efforts were made for interaction of the distant students through telephone and fax. In case of fax questions, the messages were received outside the telelecture studio. On the whole, telelectures were heard attentively.

Non Government Organisation

A number of non government organisations, like Self Employed Women's Association (SEWA), Ahemedabad, Women's Action Group (AWAG), Agha Khan Rural Support Programme (AKRSP), UNICEF, Child Relief and You (CRY), use this technology to educate, update and enhance the competency of their target population.

Conclusion

Educational broadcast and the small media like the films, filmstrips, etc. have a fairly long history in Indian education. Interactive television, in that comparison, is of recent origin. It can be traced back only in the early 1990s. Hence, its history is as brief as a little more than a decade. It has, however, shown some important promises. Firstly, it has been extremely resilient; beginning with two-way audio, popularly known as Talk-Back, it switched over to one-way video and two-way audio by the end of 1990s. Within a span of less than 5 years, it has adapted to two-way video conferencing and virtual classroom modality. This technological development and adaptiveness can also be examined against the adaptation of this technology in business and industries like BEL, etc. Compared to industrial adaptation one must admit educational adaptation has been relatively slow.

Although large number of institutions have come forward to use interactive TV medium of delivery of programmes through distance mode, the learner-response is not very encouraging. Given the choice, not many participate in the virtual classrooms. Similarly, many of the interactive sessions do not generate enough interactivity. It seems, teachers at the teaching end studio, adapt the same strategies and styles of teaching as practised in the formal classrooms. The learners at the distant end also demonstrate their culture of passivity. This substantially reduces the gains that could have been achieved through interactivity. The cultural attributes and syndromes of conventional education also restrict interactive television.

There is, however, a very strong hope of this medium. Interactive television has become part and parcel of main frame medium. News, cultural programmes, TV debates build-in such interactions through two-way video and/or one-way telephone conversation and SMS facility of mobile phones. Indian people are continuously exposed to this media and witness its live demonstration everyday. With a highly technology appreciative young community that India is and expanding network of two-way video conferencing facilities, particularly with the launching of EDUSAT, Interactive TV is poised for a big leap into the future.

5

Educational Satellite

International Experiences

Introduction

Satellite Communication for education is used the world over. Use of satellite and Interactive Television broadcasts are used in countries where geography and demography make it difficult to provide efficient formal education. Accordingly, many innovations have been tried out.

This chapter attempts to trace the development of television and satellite broadcast around the world. Little coverage is given to radio broadcasts. The data have been collected from various websites and printed literature. The authors have made a few attempts to provide a detailed listing of the history and the development in the use of satellite in education. Whatever information is available, is scattered, except for some recent publications, which give comprehensive information about educational media in some commonwealth countries. (Reddi and Mishra 2005, Reddi 2003, etc.). An attempt has been made here to present experiences of use of satellite in education in various countries in the world.

The chapter also provides case studies/experiments of

the use of satellite in education. I must hasten to add that the experiments quoted here are not the only experiments conducted by the respective countries. There are many others. I have just presented a few important ones. I also tried to find out the impact of these experiments on the learners, but no research evidences on the effectiveness and success of these experiments could be laid hands on. Before we move on to present the country cases, it would be useful to review the Joint Information Systems Committee (JISC) review. JISC provides strategic guidance, advice and opportunities to use ICT to support teaching, research and administration.

JISC (www.jisc.ac.uk/sat-report42.html) in its report has described the applications of satellite technology in education. The uses of various types are listed in the box:

Type	*Short Description*
Broadcast	Common use of satellite technology where complete educational programmes are broadcast to large number of potential learners.
Interactive	A mixed media service where satellite is used for one-
Television	way delivery of educational material and other interactive systems used for the return link from the learner
Data Broadcast	One-way communication networks offering to the end-user data, such as video files, website contents, applications and any other form of information that can be digitally stored.
Internet	Use of satellite technology where complete educational

Type	*Short Description*
Access	programmes are broadcast to large number of potential learners.
One-and	Satellite technology is used by providers to offer
Two-Way	one-or two-way high speed IP connectivity via satellite
Internet Satellite Access	to individual end-users.
VSAT Network	Private satellite networks often used in the commercial world to provide entire commercial networks.

China

Radio and Television are the two main media for delivering teaching programmes in China. Radio and television programmes are used in China both at the school as well as higher education levels. It started with higher education programmes in 1960, when television broadcasting began to develop. During 1960-66, more than 8000 students graduated from Beijing Television University (TVU). But there was a Cultural Revolution during 1966-76 and the initiatives taken were interrupted. In 1979, China's Central Radio and Television University was set up in Beijing.

The Peoples Republic of China (PRC) launched its first satellite, known as China-1 or Mao-1 in April 1970. The launch made China the fifth nation with a space rocket. But China's space industry picked up its pace in 1980s and 1990s. In 1981, PRC launched three satellites to orbit with one rocket. The Long, March-2 rocket, which carried China's first homing satellite to orbit, was launched in 1975. During 1980s China sold commercial space launchers to foreign satellite owners. For example, China launched Pakistan's first satellite Badr-A in 1990. Badr-A after 146 days in space fell into the atmosphere. China carried Indonesian satellite Palapa-B2 and Western Unions Westar 6 satellite to orbit in 1984. By the end of 2001, China had launched 50 satellites with 90 per cent success rate. By 2006 China is planning to launch at least 35 different science and application satellites (Space Today Online, 2003). These satellites are referred by different names in China. Like China's communication satellite is known as Dongfanghong (DFH), the oceanography satellites are known as Haiyan (HY-1 and HY-2) and so on. These satellites will be used for communications and direct-to-home broadcasting, meteorological and oceanographic observations, navigation and positioning, disaster mitigation, and seed breeding. China has also planned to launch a manned spacecraft like USA and Russia.

There are number of experiments conducted by China using satellite, but an important experiment in the field of education is presented in the box.

Chinese Education TV

China's Central Radio and TV University (CCRTVU) is a dedicated distance education institution, which offers multimedia university courses through radio, TV, print, audio-visual materials and computer software. It is located in Beijing under the direct supervision of the State Education Commission (SEDC). The CCRTVU, together with 28 Provincial TV Universities (PRTVU), was set up in 1979.

At present, this distance education system is made up of the CCRTVU, 44 PRTVUs, more than 690 branch schools at prefecture and city level, 1,600 study centres at county level and 13,000 teaching classes. The system is run and operated at different levels, both central and local, based on overall planning with the CCRTVU as its centre.

On 1 July 1986, China Educational TV (CETV) was founded and it began to transmit CCRTVU's courses via satellite. It has now three channels available to transmit programmes, mainly the CCRTVU's own courses. At the beginning, CCRTVU's courses were transmitted for 33 teaching hours per week nationwide via the microwave network of the CCTV.

At the moment, the total number of programmes transmitted via both CCTV and CETV per year amounts to about 9,000 teaching hours. Meanwhile, local TV and radio stations also transmit some of the CCRTVU's courses as well as local TVU's courses. Chinese Education TV experiment is one-way video broadcast via satellite with return via various media. SinaSat-1 from Sino Satellite Communications Company Limited covers all of China.

The CCRTVU system has become an important component in China's higher education system. It makes great contributions not only in extending the scale of higher education by training a large number of qualified professional personnel for economic construction and social development, but also in adjusting the disciplines for higher education and improving the imbalance in the geographical distribution of higher education in China.

Source: www.jisc.ac.uk/sat-report42.html

Canada

Canada has a dual system of broadcasting. The Canadian Broadcasting Corporation (CBC) provides a comprehensive national broadcast service in Canada. Most communities in Canada have the CBC radio and television services in French as well as in English. The school radio in Canada began in 1942 by the CBC. The first experimental schools TV broadcast was launched in 1954. It was an 8-part series called *Lets Take A Look*. There was another experiment done in 1956 which was a set of 15 programmes reaching over 60,000 students all over the country. The regular schools TV broadcasts were scheduled in 1960. These programmes were oriented to large scale national interest subjects which were relevant to all irrespective of local curriculum requirements. Several provinces like Manitoba and Nova Scotia did their own regular schools programmes, co-produced by CBC. Some of the provinces also conducted instructional TV programmes for specialized teachers. The CBC programmes, were primarily enrichment programmes rather than instructional programmes.

Canada launched its first satellite, Alouette I in 1962. With the launch of this satellite, Canada became the third nation in 1962 to have built its own satellite for orbit. During this decade the other types of satellites launched were-Alouette – ISIS satellites and the Black Brand rockets. With these satellites, it was possible to deliver television programmes in English and French to the whole country. In 1967, Canada's space programme, refocused on satellite applications. In 1972, Canada launched Anik A1. NASA launched it on Thor-Delta launch vehicle and Canada became the first nation to have a domestic satellite in geostationary orbit; Anik A2 was launched in 1973 as a backup, and Anik A3 was kept on the ground till 1975. With the Anik A satellites, the quality telephone service and television programme reached every region in the country. Telesat Canada introduced satellite services on commercial basis; the communications Research Center of DOC developed new communications satellite technology and new users. Communications Technology Satellite (CTS) was an experimental programme jointly sponsored by NASA. DOC supplied the earth stations. Their earth stations were very flexible as they were quickly installed and were easy to operate by the users. Many educational programmes were telecast through Anik through out Ontario. In 1979, the Government of Canada supported another series, Anik B, which was the second-generation satellite launched by Telesat Canada. Knowledge Network-an educational channel-was set up in British Columbia. With these two satellites, Canada was seen as a world leader in the use of satellites for social services, especially for health and education. Presently, the Anik C and Anik D series have been replaced by two Anik E's. In Canada satellite systems have been adapted to serve educational needs of many provinces. British Columbia, Alberta, Saskatchewan, Manitoba and Quebec, each have a dedicated satellite channel and Ontario has two, one for English and second for French language. Medical specialists use television via the satellite. Night school students in British Columbia also receive lectures from an Institute of Technology in Vancouver.

The Pacific Region

The Pacific Ocean is a region of various cultures and inhabitants. People in the region speak more than 1200 languages. Radio was the first media to go to the island territories. In the South Pacific region, broadcasting was derived from British, French and American origins. The Pacific region has conducted many experiments in educational broadcasting, particularly educational television in American Samoa. It used NASA's satellite ATS-1 for educational experiments using low cost ground stations. Radio in the Pacific was introduced not to provide mass communications to the inhabitants but to enable the colonial settlers to gain access to news from home, to get weather forecast etc. Technology improved and cheap transistor radio receivers were in use. As the islands in Pacific are separated by vast distances, the South Pacific Commission (SPC), which is an inter-governmental technical assistance body, was active in the field of broadcasting since 1970. The SPC produced programmes on pacific music, stories and legends, news programme, etc. It emphasized on training the member countries which were becoming independent and wished to replace expatriate personnel in their radio stations with nationals. Later in 1973, Johnston advocated that all Pacific territories should introduced closed circuit TV that is video-replay systems. He also advocated a regional consortium to supervise the introduction of broadcast television. His recommendations influenced governments, like Fiji.

The largest experiment in educational broadcasting in the South Pacific was the educational television in American Samoa (Schramm et. al. 1967, Schramm 1977, Rochstad and McMillan 1978). The experiment was to restructure the whole school system by means of television. Six VHF television channel stations were installed with four studio production centres capable of producing 200 television lessons a week. Television was the major form of instruction for six elementary school grades and high school grades. Studio teachers presented television programmes. Teachers also prepared written materials for use in the classrooms. Teachers were producing 6000 live programmes a year (Schramm 1977). But in 1971 these programmes were cut to some 2,200 live programmes per year. However, parents, teachers and political leaders criticized the television programmes. Schramm et. al., (1981) found a negative relationship between favorable opinion of instructional television and experience with it in the year 1972-76. In 1975, live programmings for schools came to an end and television was removed from school curriculum. Among the many experiments, the Pan Pacific and Communication Experiments by Satellite programme is worth mentioning here.

Pan Pacific and Communication Experiments by Satellite

The Pan Pacific and Communication Experiments by Satellite (PEACESAT) programme is now celebrating its 40 years in the Pacific Islands. The programme started in 60s when in 1963, the first geostationary communication satellite was launched. In 1966, NASAs Application Technology Satellite (ATS-1) was launched to conduct weather information experiments. In 1971, Dr Bystrom proposed the PEACESAT project to NASA, which was approved. The proposal was to demonstrate the benefits of currently available telecommunication technology when applied specifically to the needs of sparsely populated areas by University of Hawaii at Manoa, at Hilo, Maui Community College, Wellington Polytechnic and the University of South Pacific. The PEACESAT network supported 100 earth stations and incorporated more sub-networks. In 1987, the PEACESAT programme was re-established under the US Department of Commerce, which approved PEACESATs use of GOES-3 satellite in 1989. In 1993, it was referred as digital PEACESAT. The PEACESAT network grew to include 53 earth stations in 22 Pacific Islands by 1996.

The main attraction of the PEACESAT services is the videoconferencing. It also supports data services such as access to the Internet. Programme areas supported are: distance learning and training, telehealth/telemedicine and research. Presently, PEACESAT is using GOES-7 satellite. Current services include interactive video and voice teleconferencing and access to Internet. PEACESAT has survived 40 years.

Source: www.jisc.ac.uk/sat-report42.html

Africa

Most of the African States attained independence by 1960 when the educational facilities were inadequate and large sections of the population were illiterate. Most of the independent African countries decided to give top priority to provide education for all. Most of the countries also realized that conventional methods could not improve the quality of education. Hence, broadcasting was thought to be the only possibility of reaching the unreached. The first radio broadcast station in Africa was started in Algeria in 1925 followed by Egypt in 1926 and Kenya in 1928. Radio stations were introduced by Colonial powers. However, television was slow in making inroads in Africa. Many countries did not have facilities for television broadcasting. Reason was high cost programme production, absence of electric power in rural Africa etc. Till today, radio is the most dominant electronic mass medium in Africa.

The African states did not restrict the broadcasting to formal education, but used it in non-formal and adult education. Most of the African states have a schools broadcasting department. Broadcast in formal education is aimed at supplementing classroom teaching. These programmes emphasized those aspects of a subject, which the classroom teacher was not capable of handling, e.g., language teaching in primary schools, social studies for secondary schools, etc. The pattern of broadcast was 15 minutes of broadcast followed by classroom discussion. Some examples are:

- The Ghana Broadcasting Corporation was started in 1957 and television was introduced to school broadcasting in 1965. By 70's there were seven subjects broadcast over television. Television offered English literature, geography, general science and mathematics and teaching methods to secondary schools and teacher training colleges.

- In Ethiopia, the Educational Television came into being in 1965. The first broadcast was in Physics followed by English lessons. Initially, the services were limited to Addis Ababa, the capital, but later, these were extended to other cities. Other courses covered were French, geography, biology, health and physics for primary and secondary classes.
- The Ivory Coast and Niger decided to use television for direct teaching in order to introduce innovations and also expand educational opportunity. In Ivory Coast, ETV comes under the Ministry of Primary and Television Education. The aim was to expand primary school enrolment and to train teachers who will need to carry new responsibility. The ETV produced seven to eight and half hours of television programmes a week. Research conducted on Ivory Coast experience indicates that the programmes were judged as a great success with high cost. There was a negative reaction from teachers who wanted to do the actual teaching themselves and resisted the idea of becoming more dependent on the medium. The Niger project was small as compared to Ivory Coast. Also, it did not use trained teachers; instead it used monitors who were given a three-month training. Both countries pointed out a marked fall in the dropout rate and significant educational achievement (1999). Later the Ivory Coast completely abandoned its ETV programme due to economic reasons and Niger met the same fate.

- In the last few years there has been a substantial growth of satellite based broadcasting in Africa. In 1995, South Africa launched the world's first digital direct-to-home subscriber satellite service known as Mindset Network to tackle country's educational and health care problems. Presently, the channel is targeting grade 10,11 and 12 learners and educators and focussing on mathematics, science and English. A time-tabled curriculum-based programme is broadcast in the morning. Late afternoons are allowed for school and home viewing. The broadcasts run from 8.30am to 5.30pm on weekdays. The network also provides the equipment, training and support for people to be able to access the content. The equipment includes a television, satellite dish decoder and video recorder. Mindset Network is planning to have two more education channels-one for early high school and other for early childhood development.

African Virtual Classroom (AVU) is an example, which combines one-way broadcasting with a synchronous and asynchronous return channel via either telephone or online chat. The AVU service footprint via New Skies Satellites (NSS) does not cover all of Africa equally well. The AVU has a core commitment to enable greater access to higher education for African students using modern Information and Communications Technologies (ICT). The strategy involves a more focused and African-based operation committed to overcoming the constraints that limit access to quality tertiary distance learning opportunities in Africa.

The AVU began its pilot operations in 1997. By 2003, 31 AVU Learning Centres (LCs) have been established in 17 sub-

Saharan countries in Africa. During this pilot phase AVU delivered some 3,000 hours of instructional programmes, registered over 23,000 students in semester-long courses, provided 1,000 personal computers to learning centres, and provided a range of other services to its members. In addition to courses, AVU offers a digital library with 2,000 full-text journals and a catalogue of subject-related web links, as well as a website, which functions as a portal and currently receives over 1 million hits on average per month, with over 45,000 active email accounts and other web-based services. The AVU infrastructure currently consists of a broadcast network with the uplink at Netsat express hub New York, USA and multiple receive-only sites (AVU learning centres) spread across Sub-Saharan Africa. This network utilizes digital video and audio broadcast over the NSS 7 in C-band.

A flexible, mixed-mode delivery approach has been adopted, in recognition of the learner environment in which AVU operates. This approach uses a careful combination of synchronous video broadcasting, online materials, pre-packaged learning materials on CD-ROMs and DVD as well as synchronous chat sessions. Interaction between the learner and the lecturer is primarily by email, and by online chats during synchronous lecture sessions. Students also have access to online chat sessions and discussion forums with their teaching assistant throughout their programmes. All tuition emanates from the learning centres. Students are expected to register at the learning centre before attending specifically scheduled synchronous sessions. AVU LCs are supervised by trained facilitators. These are individuals who are familiar with the subject matter being taught and are mature enough to assist students during synchronous and asynchronous sessions. The facilitators are always in close consultation with the lecturer and teaching-assistant teams. While the first two phases of the development of the AVU have been successfully accomplished, the third phase of the AVU consists of developing a full two-way audio and video communication network. The AVU will achieve this through the deployment of VSAT systems with integrated videoconferencing, video-streaming, Video-on-Demand and VOIP (Voice over IP) technologies. (*Source*: www.jisc.ac.uk/sat-report42.html)

Teletuks

Teletuks is an Interactive Television service. Teletuks is a community-based project and broadcasts currently beams, via digital satellite, to 72 schools in the four inland provinces, namely Gauteng, Northern, Northwest and Mpumalanga. These schools are mostly located in rural areas although some townships' schools have also been equipped using sponsorship money. The transmissions can be viewed at any of the more than 72 viewing venues across the country or by anyone who has access to DSTV at home. Synchronous or asynchronous interactivity is possible as students can give feedback by phone, fax or email. The formal university programmes also include print-based materials. As a community service, Teletuks also televises school lessons to senior secondary learners in an endeavour to help address some of the educational needs of the country and to help prepare potential students for the demands of tertiary study.

It is a free service aiming to supplement what educators do at schools by giving extra tuition in the 'killer subjects' like Mathematics, Physical Science, Biology, English, Geography and Accounting. Career Guidance and Primary Health Care slots are integrated as well, dealing with issues likes AIDS awareness and even ways of becoming involved in playing professional rugby. The intention of the programme is not to replace educators at schools, but to assist learners preparing for their final school-leaving exam in the more difficult aspects of the particular subject. The lessons are generic and aim to review, rather than to introduce new content. Logistics, however, prevent supply of support material. The programme is currently aimed at senior learners aged 16/18 (Grades 11 & 12) who can watch 50-minute lessons in two subjects, four afternoons a week of the academic year. The lesson schedule is prepared a term in advance and sent to schools where the designated facilitator is expected to notify learners and make further arrangements regarding accessibility and operation of equipment. Apart from the weekly lessons, a winter and spring school is also scheduled during July and October school holidays. A total of 30 hours per subject is screened annually. The providers of Teletuks argue that as a mass medium, television is more accessible to the average learner than computer technology. Within rural areas, learners are also more likely to make a personal investment in satellite technology which could be shared by the community rather than buy a PC that has a dedicated application.

The University of Pretoria has a history of investing in sophisticated educational technological applications. The Department of Telematic Learning and Education Innovation has used satellite transmissions, electronic networks, the Internet, and its virtual campus, to supplement traditional undergraduate and postgraduate teaching for the past 7 years. Such innovations not only support flexible, life-long learning, but also make it possible to provide high-quality education to learners, many in remote areas, who cannot be accommodated in traditional face-to-face teaching scenarios. The niche markets, which the interactive transmissions serve, are students enrolled for courses in the fields of education, nursing, African languages and some modules in other faculties.

Source: www.jisc.ac.uk/sat-report42.html

Australia

Public service broadcasting in Australia is the responsibility of a federal body. Australia has a commercial and non-commercial broadcast systems. Australia has two services. One is Australian Broadcasting Commission (ABC) and another is Special Broadcasting Service (SBS). Schooling in Australia is the responsibility of each state. ABC School Broadcasts Advisory Committees were established in each state in early 1930s. By 1935, 21 per cent of all Australian schools were making regular use of radio programmes, which increased to 90 per cent in mid 1950s. ABC also produced booklets to supplement the radio programmes which were distributed free to the students.

Television was introduced in 1956. Kindergarten Playtime, the first TV experimental educational programme was introduced in 1956. In 1960, a concerted effort was made to plan series of programmes for use nationwide. Production facilities for educational purposes were expanded in 1963 and 1964. Direct teaching programmes were introduced in science and mathematics to help implement new syllabi in these subjects and to overcome an acute shortage of mathematics and science teachers. By 1969, the Education Department of South Australia and Queensland had begun to equip their schools with video recorders. By 1972, 90 per cent of all Australian schools were making regular use of school television programmes. The school broadcast consisted of wide range of both enrichment and subject specific programmes. Supplementary printed materials for both teachers and students were available for many of the radio and television schools broadcasts.

ABCs Schools Television also provides resources for students and teachers. Interactive television technologies are used to link schools and teachers on a region wide basis. The main feature of the transmissions is the capacity to use the government Westlink service to distribute teaching and learning programmes. These programmes are transmitted for four hours each week using satellite system that provides for one-way video and two-way audio. Australia also uses interactive television in Victoria. It also uses broadcast television for its remote communities. The Open Learning Development Services within the Open Access Support Center in Queensland, deploys VHF and UHF television transmitters and receivers to deliver programmes to remote rural communities.

Australian satellite system was started in 1985 with Aussat-1 and 2 of the first generation of satellites. The downlink has two national beams and four spot beams covering different parts of the country. Aussat-3 have a beam with uplink and downlink capacity available for the Southwest Pacific region. The frequencies used were around 14-12 GH3 so as to be free of any interference with the microwave links on the ground. Among the few experiments were the Queensland Government's satellite network 'Q-NET' which involves broadcast television to about 30 centers. This project looked into whether satellite communication is a cost-effective means of providing postgraduate vocational teaching and continuing medical education to general practitioners in Queensland. A two-year pilot phase of the project seeks to provide an in-service course to pre-school to year three teachers to help them develop children's reading and writing abilities. There are different types of earth stations: Interactive, which can receive television broadcasts and data and voice transmissions as well as transmit data and voice television, receive only TVRO which can only get television, data and voice but cannot transmit signals to the satellite. This was the first Tele course development in Australia. The Darling Downs Institute of Advanced Education, Toowoomba, runs another imaginative distance education programme in Australia. The Institute offers a wide variety of courses leading to diplomas and degrees in electrical, civil and mechanical engineering and accounting, education and educational administration.

Centrelink Education Network

Centrelink Education Network is an example of one-way broadcast of television programmes with a return support channel via terrestrial lines. Centrelink uses the Optus B3 satellite for broadcasting of all their programmes. Centrelink has nearly 400 customer service locations throughout Australia, many in remote and rural locations. It currently has 371 sites equipped and connected to the satellite network. All customer service staff has access to a training room with equipment installed either in their own office or in a site nearby. There are 2,017 keypads connected to this system. The network covers 7,692,024 sq km area. The Centrelink Education Network has, as its main delivery platform, a state-of-the-art interactive distance-education facility, fully integrating video, voice and data to deliver live, real-time training and education to 24,000 staff members of 20 different government agencies across Australia. It is a two-way voice and one-way video system, i.e. a one-way broadcast with a return support channel via terrestrial lines. The student response keypad uses a telephone line to enable the facilitator and participant to talk to each other. Interactivity occurs in a number of ways. For example, a student can respond to pre-determined questions or he/she may ask the presenter for clarification on issues raised during the lesson.

Centrelink offers a blended solution to their education programmes, most of which are accredited to match nationally recognised qualifications. Prior to participating in the satellite-enabled learning, students may undertake an online Learning Needs Analysis to determine their skill gaps or learning needs. They then download workbooks and other materials from the Intranet for pre-reading, or they may watch a CD-ROM from their desktops. After a learning session, they may have face-to-face group discussions to relate their learning to the workplace.

For the satellite broadcasts, programmes of about

45 minutes duration are produced from the Centrelink Canberra studios and travel by satellite to Centrelink offices across the country. Employees log-on to the learning session via a student response keypad, using an Australian Government Service number. This allows the system to recognise each employee and their work location and provides accurate management information on the amount and type of training each employee undertakes. Support is provided in a number of ways. All learning programmes broadcast over the network are accompanied by a workbook that is available electronically and this often provides extra information for participants. All programmes are based on adult learning principles and an instructional design that uses the best mix of information delivery and interactivity. The network uses internal expertise such as subject matter experts who appear on camera from the Canberra studios or remotely through the voice recognition system.

Pre-recorded videos and DVDs are used to enhance the programmes and these can be played after the programme to review information. An email facility is also available to learners if they want more information after the programme. All emails received are responded to within a short timeframe. In the actual work location, support can be provided by an office subject expert or trainer or team leader.

All Centrelink Education Network programmes are live and interactive. For each new lesson, there are a number of broadcasts depending on the size of the target audience. For large initiatives, this can be as many as 50. While video copies of all programmes are kept, staff are encouraged to use the video tapes only for 'refresher' purposes and not as the main source of learning, as evidence suggests that adults learn best by interaction. A 'video on demand' system is available where students can request a copy of the programme to view or review after the live programme.

Source: www.jisc.ac.uk/sat-report42.html

New Zealand

In New Zealand there is a single Department of Education and nationwide public service broadcasting organization. 780 radio broadcast programmes were produced annually by 1973. In 1974, the production of schools broadcast shifted from Radio NZ to the Department of Education. During 1974-79, the Schools Broadcasts Section of RNZ was run down and studios for the departments own audio production unit were not commissioned until 1981. Radio New Zealand's schools related broadcasts comprise ten-minute news programmes for pre schoolers and 20 minutes programme each day for the correspondence school. There was also a proposal to replace the schools radio broadcasts by the distribution of materials on audiocassettes. The New Zealand Correspondence School began broadcasting to its pupils in 1931. The 1982 broadcasts, 279 programmes, comprised 45 hours of original programming and 12 hours of repeats. In addition 9,000 students received audiocassettes as part of their courses. In 1982, the school ventured into television. The Correspondence School radio broadcasts are no longer designed as formal lessons but as enrichment materials.

Television New Zealand (TVNZ) caters for the under 5's with Play School; a 25 minute programme presented twice daily "Sesame Street" was first broadcast in 1970 in NZ for entertainment purpose. New Zealand produces programmes for adults, like Money Programme and Computer Programme.

United Kingdom

In United Kingdom, British Broadcasting Corporation (BBC) provides quality educational resources to all levels of people. These resources include radio and television broadcasts. Radio broadcasts for schools in UK had been run since 1924. Number of innovative school radio series in different areas has been produced. Along with the programmes, School Radio provides a practical range of teachers notes, students pamphlet's etc. to support the broadcast. BBC also broadcasts Continuing Education Radio Programmes for adult learners. Listening of the programmes is combined with books and cassettes. School Television is inspiring the British schools for the last forty-five years. The TV programmes are produced for the schools keeping in mind the challenges of the new curriculum. The programmes are produced in consultation with teachers, trainers, viewers and listeners across the UK. School TV programmes promote active viewing with programmes leading to creative follow up activity like research, problem solving, discussion, reading and writing. Educational programmes are also produced for adult learners.

BBC has a Broadcasting Research department, which was set up as early as 1936. It provides audience reactions to both TV and radio output. The research findings are used for strategic planning. UK has other alternative broadcast services like Channel Four, Central Independent Television and The Leaning Channel (TLC) which broadcast ITV programmes. The schools in UK can use either BBC or any other service provider. The details of all these channels are not described here but the important point is that in UK there are educational channels other than BBC, which broadcast educational programmes.

The Open University in Britain, established in 1971, broadcasts lectures on BBC television. The programmes are broadcast on the BBCs national radio and television networks. The programmes are for undergraduate or non-degree programmes and have a reach of more than ten million viewers. These programmes cover a wide range of subjects and are filmed all over the world. These television programmes are found to be effective and useful.

JISC & UKERNA 2-way Satellite Access Trial project is a two-way satellite Internet access. This pilot project operated from November 2002 until the end of April 2004. It involves 17 higher or further education sites in the UK, all located in areas described as being rural and/or remote. These areas are unable to receive ADSL or Cable Modem broadband services, and include locations in the Highlands and Islands of Scotland, Cornwall and Wales.

The aim of this trial was to investigate how far satellite telecommunication technology can contribute towards solving connectivity and access problems in remote and currently undeserved areas. Seventeen off-campus learning centres, off-campus sites and individuals (staff) were equipped with small VSAT-based systems and services to assess the feasibility of broadband satellite as a technology for Internet access.

Two satellite service providers, representing three major satellite telecommunications technology providers, have taken part in this trial. The user group is divided into two application areas, one focusing on connecting off-campus learning centres, small user-groups and individual users (1 to 4 PCs per site), the other focuses on providing Internet connectivity for larger sites (10 PCs per site). The aim of the trial is to evaluate to what extent two-way satellite can effectively provide last-mile broadband connectivity. The results of the trial evaluation show an increasingly satisfied user base, certainly after initial network problems have been ironed out. This has resulted in a take up of over 50 per cent of the commercial VSAT offer within the pilot user group. Although the usage is relatively small (traffic rarely exceeds 1 GB per month per client station), users acknowledge the fact that in their location, they do not expect an alternative access method within the foreseeable future. Moreover, this technology is providing them with an opportunity to adopt innovative Learning and teleworking methods, that were simply not possible with the previously available access provision.

On the basis of the final evaluation, JISC will consider whether it will offer or recommend a satellite-based service to its user community. (*Source*: www.jisc.ac.uk/sat-report42.html)

Space Link Education Satellite

The Space Link Satellite will be world's first satellite, which is solely designed and dedicated to education (www.spacelink.org.uk/content/). This satellite will enable the students worldwide to make observations in space and perform quality of experiments and other space related activities at a low cost

The Space Link Bearing Foundation is a registered UK charity. The aim of the Foundation is to provide means to motivate students towards science and engineering subjects and also provide new and more powerful ways of learning these subjects. It will also create a one-stop space based resource on the web for teachers. The groundbreaking part of this initiative will be the world's first purpose-built dedicated education satellite, orbiting the Earth and conducting experiments in space, relevant to the needs of the school community worldwide. The satellite will also deliver tailored data streams which can be archived and provide a source of space artifacts for use in developing new learning resources.

The Space Link satellite will be about 55-60 kgs, traveling round the Earth at 1200-1300 km altitude. It will provide a reliable, direct, one-stop service for schools through its radio signals, equipment and specially tailored data streams. Some of its equipment will be remotely re-configurable to meet teacher's requirements.

Schools will need PLs and a low cost aerial, receiver and software kit to participate in activities, which involve direct interaction with the satellite. Students will be able to perform live, hands-on classroom, laboratory and fieldwork involving the satellite as it panes overhead. Schools without their own aerial and receiver will be able to participate indirectly through their well accessed and the Space Link operations service center.

Space Link's Learning Service will provide teachers with a portfolio of teaching aids and support services to enable them to harness the learning potential of space, delivering the portfolio directly into schools PLs worldwide, at a cost affordable to schools.

The schools will be benefited in the following ways once they have access to the dedicated education satellite.

1. It will help teachers in achieving pupil motivation and challenge and in bringing the reality of the outside world directly into the classroom.
2. It will introduce new, cost effective classroom, laboratory, field and extra curricular work. The satellite will support the teaching of subjects, such as science, applications of mathematics, technology, geography and space. Some of the other subjects will be languages, business studies, engineering, history, art, music and religious studies.

Source: 2002 Spacelink, Education Satellite.

France

In France, broadcasts for adult education began in late 1952. This led to the establishment of Teleclubs in schools for the whole community to watch TV together. These were not school television programmes but fell under the auspices of the school television service for administrative purposes. The Ministry of Education in 1954, started TV programmes. These programmes were transmitted nationally on broadcasting time loaned from the Radio Television Francaise. The broadcasts were on all subjects but were dominated by English language programmes. Centre National de Documentation Pedagogique (CNDP) is another group associated with the French Ministry of Education. The group produces audio-visual materials and promotes the use of technology in education. The programmes produced are for primary and secondary schools. At present, France has three state channels: France 2, France 3 and Lacinquieme.

Les Amphis de france 5 is an example of educational programmes video broadcast via the satellites Telecom 2C from France, Hot Bird 5 (analogue) and Hot Bird 5 (digital-TPS) from Eutelsat Telecom, the ASTRA 1 H (canalsatellite) from ASTRA. Les Amphis de france 5, a French educational TV programme and website, has been operating as a service since February 1996. It allows schools, training centres and individuals to access audio-visual products and documents via a dedicated website or via television. The aim of Les Amphis de france 5 is to distribute knowledge and to provide pedagogical support, mainly to students and teachers in higher education. The programmes are also of interest to the general public, covering themes such as work, economy, sciences, art, history, literature and media. Visitors to the website will find a catalogue of 500 titles and the broadcast schedule. At the same time the website allows access to the accompanying documents, such as texts, exercises and corrections.

The TV channel france 5 is part of the France Television Group, alongside France 2 and France 3. The programme 'Les Amphis de france 5' is broadcast according to the following schedule:

- Monday mornings from 5.40 am: programmes that have been suggested by the public. For this purpose, viewers can choose from the 500 titles in the catalogue. The most requested programmes are then broadcast. This could be called a near 'video-on-demand' service.
- From Tuesday to Friday, every morning at 5.40 am: video lectures by academics from all over France. Each day covers a different subject area (science, humanities, mathematics, languages).
- On Saturdays and Sundays, every morning at 6 am: a selection of discussions and conferences.

Les Amphis de france 5 also broadcasts online via streaming as part of 'Canal U', the web TV service of French higher education establishments. Canal U consists of 10 different channels offering about 1,500 hours of educational videos. The channel 'Les Amphis de france 5' offers 130 programmes, enriched with synchronised illustrations and accompanying documents.

The programmes of Les Amphis de france 5 are available on 3 types of communication network: Terrestrial network; Cable network; and Satellite network. The programmes of France 5 distributed by satellite network are for an international audience. An estimated 14 to 20 million people watch France 5 every week, not only in France but also in the rest of Europe and North Africa. (Source: www.jisc.ac.uk/sat-report42.html).

Sat & Clic

The satellite communications infrastructure included a transmission platform and a hub located near Paris, which up-linked the educational bouquet of digital TV and Internet

IP data multiplexed in DVB/MPEG-2 standard. The signal was transmitted in broadcast mode by one high-power TPS transponder of the HotBird 3 satellite of Eutelsat to the SAT&CLIC terminals. The TV signal was decoded by set-up-box equipment. A satellite board installed in a standard PC decoded IP data. The PC could be used as a gateway to be linked to any type of local network (Categories 1, 3 and 5).

At the beginning of 1999, the Satel-IT programme was launched by the French Education, Research and Technology Ministry. In this framework, the SAT&CLIC project, running from December 1999 until June 2001, submitted by LAGARDERE Group and TPS (Television Par Satellite), had been selected to demonstrate how the space systems could help in providing interactive multimedia services for educational applications, including Internet access, cooperative work, Internet conferencing and interactive digital TV.

The SAT&CLIC project involved more than 200 educational establishments in France, including primary and secondary schools, universities, teachers training centres (IUFM) and resources centres (CNDP). The network was not expanded after June 2001 due to a lack of support from the new government.

During the project's lifetime, the LAGARDERE Group, through its media (Hachette Multimédia, educational publishers) and technology partner companies from EADS Group (ASTRIUM, EADS Telecom), had developed a global SAT&CLIC offer which included a wide spectrum of educational services and multimedia products. Internet and broadband communications technologies were used for delivery of these services and products.

Satellite technology had been chosen because it offers the following advantages: an immediate availability on a large area especially for rural areas, the same service delivered for every user in this area, and a low-cost terminal when using current DVB standard for digital TV technology. Moreover, satellite was found efficient in this educational context because it allowed multicasting data while operating in an asymmetric interactive transmission mode, which is well adapted to Internet applications such as browsing the web.

The SAT&CLIC bouquet of services included a set of IP broadcast and multicast services. They supported delivery of educational online applications and multimedia contents, developed by Hachette Multimedia, LAGARDERE group publishers (Hachette, Didier) and several associated partners. In addition, Digital TVs selected for educational purposes were provided by TPS.

SAT&CLIC provided a set of IP services, including:

- Hi-Net service providing Internet access with satellite downlink.
- Hi-Want service enabled users to request for remote loading of Internet web servers into local caches.
- Hi-Cast service supported secured data multicasting for distribution of any type of data to networked communities; applications were developed to support co-operative work between groups of teachers (Intranet), and database replication
- Hi-Channel service for data-streaming through dedicated satellite channel; applications were developed for broadcasting videoconference, live or recorded

Other IP services deal with FTP server mirroring, distribution of news feed (newsgroups) and multicast of Mbone programmes.

To take benefit from satellite transmission, and more generally from broadband telecommunication infrastructures, Hachette Multimedia provided dedicated educational applications, in collaboration with media companies of LAGARDERE Group, and many other public or private associated partners.

DIDACTUA was one of these online applications. DIDACTUA was a new multimedia service that gave access to:

- Educational services and contents associated to news events, and
- Educational libraries.

Contents, structured by 'modules', were linked to radio news, videos, TV resources, and articles from newspapers websites and other specific resources produced by publishers.

Source: www.jisc.ac.uk/sat-report42.html

Japan

Japan started its radio services for schools in 1935. These programmes were recognized as an educational aid in 1941 and were popular, as there was shortage of teaching aids such as textbooks. Nippon Hosa Kyokai (NHK) started a full-scale service for schools in 1951, before the official TV service was started. NHK started a specific educational TV channel in 1958 and the schools service was shared between this and the main channel. NHK has its own satellite-broadcasting channel. Majority of the schools at all levels make use of NHKs school programmes.

Japan's space programme began in 1955 with the contribution of a handful of university professors. In 1970, Japan became the fourth country to launch its own satellite in orbit, after the USSR, the United States and France. Japan enjoyed a 100 per cent success rate with its rockets though Japan's space agency the National Space Development Agency (NASDA) had its first failure in 20 launches in 1989 (Space Today online 2004).

i-Space Project toward Better Society

NASDA conducted two pilot experiments as part of the i-Space Project, in the fields of education, health and welfare.

First is the pilot experiment for education. This experiment tries to realize the Field Learning which is to bring such outdoor study environments as ruins and farms into classroom by making use of the satellite's feature of wide coverage.

With the use of a satellite, a teacher in the field is able to communicate with students in the classroom even from hard-to-communicate locations, such as mountainous places, where a cellular phone does not work. By transmitting the image of 360-degree from a panoramic camera, a teacher gives a lecture from the area being displayed, while providing students with the feeling of actually being there. The panoramic images will also enable teachers to educate students from a comprehensive viewpoint.

This experiment is being conducted as joint research between NASDA and the National Institute of Multimedia Education (NIME) under the Ministry of Education, Culture, Sports, Science and Technology. NASDA is mainly in charge of pre-demonstrating communication technology prior to the utilization experiment on the Engineering Test Satellite VIII (ETS-VIII).

The school appointed as a model for the experiment is Miyazaki Prefectural Gokase Secondary School, which introduces a six-year educational system. Miyazaki University will cooperate in evaluating the educational effectiveness of the experiment.

The use of satellite earth observation data in education is also encouraged in this experiment. One application example is a study on an environmental issue, in which the experiment equipment is used in the place with an environmental problem, and the report from this site is compared in the classroom with the data observed by earth observation satellite.

A remote tour of the Tsukuba Space Center was conducted from the school classroom on January 17, 2001, with the aim of demonstrating the usefulness of the system. A question and answer session was held after explanations of the Space Center and the artificial satellites. Many questions were received from the students and a lively demonstration ensued. The feature of the experiment system, which transmits panoramic images, instead of a teleconference system, made students feel that they were actually at the Space Center.

A lecture and exchange class from Tomisima High School in Hyuga, Miyazaki Prefecture, is planned in March this year. In the next fiscal year, the experiment will be expanded to include students in schools within Japan and overseas. Based on the experiment results, further efforts will be taken to make such field lectures more practical using handy communication terminal through the ETS-VIII utilization experiment.

Source: www.jisc.ac.uk/sat-report42.html

Global Development Learning Network (GDLN)

The Global Development Learning Network (GDLN) is a global partnership of learning centers that use advanced information and communication technologies to connect people around the world (www.gdln.org). GDLN offers videoconferencing and Internet resources for communication. Academic institutions, development agencies government agencies and non government organizations use the services of GDLN. World Bank established GDLN and till day it is providing support to the Network.

The GDLN network uses a mix of satellites covering Africa, the Americas, Eastern Europe and Asia and is an example of a VSAT network being used in an educational context.

The Global Development Learning Network (GDLN) established by the World Bank is a partnership of public, private and non-governmental organisations providing a fully interactive, multi-channel network with a mandate to serve the developing world. GDLN partner organisations work together to take advantage of the most modern of technology, for building local capacity, sharing learning and knowledge, and building a global community dedicated to reducing poverty. The mission of GDLN is 'to harness modern technology-including interactive video, the Internet, and satellite communications-in a cost-effective way, so that people who know are brought together with those who need to know, to learn with and from each other about the full range of development issues'. Network connectivity is achieved through a Very Small Aperture Terminal (VSAT) satellite transmission system for voice, video and data. A total of three satellites provide coverage to Africa and the Americas, Eastern Europe and Asia. GDLN uses Intelsat over the Atlantic to cover Africa and Latin America, using a technology called DAMA (Demand Assigned Multiple Access). Over Europe and parts of Central Asia they use Orion and over South Asia and East Asia they use an IOR satellite from an uplink in Perth. GDLN connects with Perth by fiber from Washington. In this way, the whole system is one satellite hop. The whole network is currently being converted to IP.

The GDLN network involves a growing consortium of facilities with high-quality interactive video conferencing and Internet capacity which is currently linking more than 50 countries in Europe, Africa, Asia, Latin America and North America. GDLN grew out of the successful pilot programme 'World Bank Learning Network', which has been under development since 1997 and relied on the Bank's high-capacity communications system.

GDLN network has now more than 70 affiliates, which are located in the developing countries. These are owned and managed by partner institutions and can accommodate upto 60 people. During 2003-2004, GDLN facilitated more than 850 videoconferencing based activities, connecting an estimated 26,000 people around the world.

Conclusion

The review of the international experience provides an interesting learning opportunity to those countries that are now getting ready to enter into the satellite based education. There are certain common features. Firstly, satellite communication was pressed into education in almost all countries to reach out to people in rural and difficult situations. It began with the industrially developed countries who's commitment to equality of opportunity is an articulated policy. Their success and support paved the way for the developing and the underdeveloped countries, particularly Africa and Asia. Secondly, almost all countries moved from broadcast to interactive television. This is an important development since its driving force is pedagogy-interactivity is the key to higher order cognition and adult learning. Thirdly, almost all countries prefered to use both receive-only and interactive channels.

One important feature of the international experience is the transition and progression from country specific educational delivery and intervention to cross country and global delivery. The programmes delivered by some of the Eurpean Countries, eg, UK and France, are accessible to large number of countries. World Bank's GDLN is a global network.

Finally, the international experience offers a platter full of learning opportunities for choice of technology, ground segment network development, software, pedagogical options, and modes and methods of assessment of impact on learning.

6

Research in Educational Media

Introduction

The Indian history of research in educational media spans over almost 45 years. The Indian studies on educational media have been reviewed by several researchers (Kulkarni and Kapadia (1974), Shah, Mehta and Kulkarni (1978), Mishra (1986), Mukhopadhyay (1989), Shukla (1991), Mukhopadhyay and Sinha, (1993), Parhar, (1993) and Dewal (1997). Internationally the reviews are written by Schramm (1977), Chu and Schramm (1987), Seels et. al. (2001). Mukhopadhyay 1989 analyzed more than 40 studies in the field of educational media. He stated that "there is a wide divergence in terms of provisions of audio visual aids in different states in the country. Even within the same state, such divergence is observable among different levels of education, namely school and higher education. Another common finding is the poor utilization of audio-visual aids across all levels of education and across the states but media programmes in education are generally popular. Students get interested in the programmes though the programmes are grossly underutilized". On the basis of these findings, Mukhopadhyay suggested 'to develop a management system including monitoring and evaluation'. Dewal (1997) reviewed studies in the area of video and ETV programmes in the Fifth Survey of Research. He reported 22 studies in these areas during 1988-92 and expressed that "most of the studies were comparative studies and spawned sterile results. The media comparison studies do not lead us anywhere. Comparison must be of one mix of methods with another mix of methods. Researches in the area of media need to be taken up not to suggest any solution but as a troubleshooting step".

Schramm (1977) in his comprehensive review found that student receiving television as a supplement to normal teaching scored higher on various attainment tests than students not viewing the programmes. This review also reveals that television instruction has been used with greater success in the lower grades than in higher schools or colleges. Johnson (1987) found that television can teach in a stand-alone format but it can teach more effectively when utilised by a competent teacher who can integrate television in the curriculum, prepare students, extend and elaborate on content, encourage viewing and provide feedback.

Clark (2001) in his book, *Learning from Media* concluded that there are no learning benefits from any specific medium or mix of media. He summarized the research on this issue in an analogy. "The best – evidence is that media are mere vehicle that deliver instruction but do not influence student achievement any more than the truck that delivers our groceries causes changes in our nutrition".

This chapter analyses the research studies on educational media in India, broadly classified into four categories:

1. Utilization of Educational Media;
2. Attitude and Reaction towards the Educational Media;

3. Effect of Media on Education; and
4. Studies on Interactive Television.

Utilization of Educational Media

Utilization studies in the developing countries have looked at resource issues from the perspective of the design and support of both educational and television systems. Seels et. al. (2001) in her review discussed that barriers to greater utilization are teachers' lack of knowledge about sources of programming for their subject matter area and research utilization. In India, the media utilization studies can be classified separately for the radio and television programmes. Interestingly, a scholar from London University did the first study on utilization. This study was a survey of the listening facilities in the schools in Bombay and Delhi. Subsequently, there have been a large number of studies on media utilization. Almost without contradiction, the Indian studies reveal rather poor utilization of educational media-both radio and television (Mukhopadhyay and Sinha, 1993). Many studies (AIR Cuttack 1972, CIET 1975, Biswal (1980), Phutela (1980), Singh and Shukla (1980), SCERT Orissa (1982), Nagaraju and Ramkumar (1982), Singh (1983), Singh and Singh (1984), Goel (1985), Sudame and Goel (1988), Singh and Umare (1986), etc.) have gone into the causes of non-utilization of radio and television. Some of the reasons repeatedly emphasised include the incompatibility of the timing of the programmes with the institutional time-table, TV sets being out of order, no seating arrangements for listening, sets not working, lack of motivation of teachers, non receipt of transmission schedules, programmes not attractive, breakdown of electricity etc. Fact remains that educational media in India is grossly underutilized.

Television programmes were also not found to be utilized at higher education level (Pillay 1992). It was found that though TV sets were provided free of cost to all the colleges, no effort was made to integrate telecast programmes with the regular time-table. It was found that the TV sets were placed either in the laboratory or library or in the hostel. In Tamil Nadu, Pillay (1992) found that almost all colleges have at least one epidiascope/slide projector/film projector/overhead projector. Blackboard, maps, charts, globes are used extensively in colleges. Reddi (1996) found out from the teachers and learners about the reasons for poor utilisation. She found that the teachers and students were reluctant in using the electronic media to improve the quality of learning. Studies by Shah (1972) and Chaudhary (1991) reported that teachers did not conduct pre and post test telecast activities and in the absence of such activities there could not be effective utilization of TV programmes.

Review of studies show that television is underutilized both at the school as well as college levels, though television is provided free of cost to all schools and colleges under the educational technology scheme.

Attitude and Reaction Towards Media

There are studies on the reaction of students and the teachers on media programmes in education. The students' reaction has been more or less positive throughout. The possible reason for the student's positive reaction is that the programmes make a break in the monotony of the conventional classroom practices. Besides, it provides an opportunity, particularly to the rural poor to listen to a media to which they may not have access at home. Students' reaction was that syllabus-based programmes should be telecast (Singh and Singh, 1984).

The teachers' reaction varied from positive to negative, through neutral. The teachers' reactions are guided by more than one consideration. On the one hand, they are able to assess the quality of the programme and compare it with their own performance in the classroom. On the other hand, the teachers, particularly the weak ones, feel threatened with the new media because the students might compare them with the radio or television teachers.

Very few institutional and individual studies have really commented on the relevance and quality of the programmes. Mohanty and Behera (1986); Singh, Prasad, Bajpai and Kaur (1984) found that the programmes telecast lack synchronization of visuals with commentary, visuals are flashed very quickly, programmes are stretched unnecessarily, and there is greater reliance on long shots.

While there have been a large number of studies on educational media, there have not been many efforts to find a breakthrough in enhancing utilization or ensuring the impact of television and radio programmes on learning. For example, one of the major conjectures is that the effect of educational programmes is not visible because of the format of the programme and poor quality. There is, interestingly, no experiment on alternative programme formats and their impact on learning. Delhi and the National Institute of Open Schooling took to production of programmes in a new format. In this format, the classrooms are simulated; students are allowed to ask questions. The video teacher responds and solves the students' problems. In a way, it is transforming the tutorial mode of instruction into the video format. This approach is still at the developmental stage and has not been tried enough to evaluate and learn from the experiences.

Effect of Media

Much research on the effects of television is contradictory or inconclusive. This does not make the research reviews useless or futile. Seels et. al. (2001) in her review discussed major theories (displacement theory, short term gratification theory, interest stimulation theory etc), methodological concerns and intervening variables vis-à-vis televisions impact on scholastic achievement. Few researchers doubt that there is a relationship between television viewing and scholastic achievement.

In India, the impact studies of media have taken two different patterns. One set of studies has tried to simulate the educational mass media into classroom, through the video and audio modes. In these studies, the experiments have been conducted on pre-test and post-test format to assess the learning outcome due to audio and video programme. As a part of the design or otherwise, almost all the studies involve an animator. Findings of the studies (Maddu 1978, Dhamija 1985, Antonysamy 1989, Idayavani 1991, Kalimuthu 1991 and Narayanasamy 1991) reveal that when video or film or other media are added and integrated with the conventional teaching, students achieve significantly higher.

The second set of studies is in the natural classroom setting where the students are actually exposed to the radio and television lessons directly. Such studies normally did not have the animator effect. The students are allowed to see the television and radio programmes, when there is actually no teacher around them.

The outcomes of studies where students are exposed directly to the television classes reveal mixed effects. In 1965-66, Neurath was invited to access the effectiveness of school broadcasts. He used an experimental design and conducted tests to see the effect of television. His conclusions were that the TV lessons provide a break in the routine and make the school more interesting. It was also found that students did better on questions that required understanding. Christiansen, an Australian observer on an educational television evaluation assignment from UNESCO reported," The outstanding elements in the Delhi Scheme are sound planning, carefully planned cooperation at all levels and thorough integration with the syllabus in the schools. The teachers were fully involved at all stages from planning to evaluation". The findings of studies (Sindhi 1963, Mangla 1967, Roy 1974, Sambooranam 1980, Kanade 1982, CET 1980, Seth 1983, Singh and Singh 1983) indicate a wide variation from no significant difference to the positive gain in learning by the students through the media.

On the other hand even year-long experiments indicate that the students exposed to subject-based television programmes, did not differ in their performance, in the tests conducted at the end of the year from those who were not exposed to the educational television programmes (*Parhar, 1993*).

Das and Das (2001) studied the viewing preferences of high school students of Doordarshan programmes. The findings of the study revealed that the students expressed interest in learning through television and video programmes. Aghi (1996) found that there was dearth of TV programmes for school children.

In India, SITE, and later INSAT, were the two largest communication experiments where satellite was used to support developmental and educational programmes. Agarwal (1978) pointed out the evaluation of SITE, which introduced satellite TV as a new medium of communication in villages of India. Shukla and Kumar (1977) conducted an extensive impact study of the SITE experiment. Results showed an improvement in language skills of the learners of the SITE exposed group. The study mainly aimed to find out changes in the behaviour and cognitive development of primary school children as a result of their exposure to television lessons. Kumar (1978) also concluded that children of the TV schools learned about personal cleanliness and social and moral values.

Mody (1978) evaluated the project and wrote "–the experiment was conceived in an era of optimism about the power of mass media, and Indian advocates of TV did not stop to ask if it was reasonable to expect the medium to shoulder such onerous responsibilities alone as if it were a magic wand'. She reports that "Disadvantaged groups such as low castes, illiterates, women and low income people gained relatively more knowledge than others who had better access to privately owned television. The SITE project was heavily oriented towards testing the hardware and technology involved".

Many other researchers studied the impact of SITE programmes (Rehman 1977, Aghi 1977, Bhaskaran 1977, Agarwal 1978, Chakaravarty 1982). These studies were conducted in various states where SITE programmes were telecast and revealed mixed results. Studies revealed that children did not understand the programmes, specially science, but they accepted the television. Research findings showed that children exposed to SITE programmes were more inquisitive, particularly during classroom teaching in General Science. The most important findings were: the technical feasibility of using the sophisticated technology in a developing country; audience favoured instructional programmes as compared to cultural programmes; gains were greater for underprivileged sections of rural society, such as females and illiterates, but expectations regarding impact were not fulfilled to the same extent; attention needed to be paid to selection of message and formative evaluation.

There are good number of studies which analysed the INSAT educational programmes. Mukhopadhyay (1989) reviewed the studies on INSAT educational programmes. He observed, "In case of INSAT programmes monitored by the CIET, it is found that most of the states do not send timely report and as a result monitoring becomes difficult. In a large number of studies, it has been found that the softwares were not totally relevant to the situation and the context. Some of the studies reflect on the language, even in case of Hindi, as the medium of the software. As an example, the Chhatisgarh region found Hindi programmes difficult to understand and un-interesting. Besides, programmes for children, specific programmes for teachers were telecast under INSAT. The aim of the programmes was to improve the competency of teachers in general". Mohanty (1992) in a study, covered all the INSAT districts of Orissa. There was apparent gain in General Science, Social Studies and Language in favour of experimental samples exposed to television.

Research Studies (Joshi 1987, Doneriya (1988), Mohanty and Rath (1990,) Sarvanam (1990), Anandan (1990), Arularam (1990), Mohanty and Sahoo 1991, Goel and Jaiswal 1992, Mohanty (1992) and Mohanty and Seth 1992) concerning the different dimensions of UGC's Countrywide Classroom ETV programmes were evaluated. The studies on the impact of UGC programmes found that majority of the programmes were understandable and content delivery rate was satisfactory. The programmes were suitable for primary target viewers i.e., students at Undergraduate level. Evaluation studies (Reddi 1997, Chaudhari 1997) have shown positive gains as a result of educational broadcasting among college students. Agarwal (1988) and Aram (1989) attempted to analyse the content of the UGC programmes using message system analysis. Studies point out that Indian made programmes should create an attitude of scientific enquiry towards solving problems. Studies on the learning outcome point out that, "whenever the media programme was preceded by the teacher with intervention, and followed by well organized discussion, the students learned better".

To sum up the impact of media on learning, Clark (1984) observed that "Learning gains come from adequate instructional design, theory and practice, not from the medium used to deliver instruction. Hence, the researchers must move from media comparison studies that yield no significant differences and begin to examine factors such as instructional design, learning theory, and theoretical frameworks which when applied to learning might account for significant difference in levels of performance."

Interactive Television

Another up-coming area of research and experimentation with the educational media is the use of interactive television. The interactive television has been used extensively since 1983 by a large number of organizations, like IGNOU, UGC, AIMA, NCERT, NIEPA, NIOS, IIT Delhi, etc.

The two centrally sponsored schemes PMOST and SOPT for in-service education of primary teachers used interactive television in the training of primary teachers in Karnataka and Madhya Pradesh in 1996. Both the experiments showed a positive impact of interactive television on learning by the teachers (Dash 1997, Prakash and Lal 1998). Dash studied the reactions of the participants on the content and its presentation, the interaction and technology whereas Prakash and Lal studied presentation and production aspects in relation to the effectiveness of the medium for orientation of primary school teachers. Phutela (1998) reported the SOPT experiment in the state of Karnataka in India. The evaluation of the experiment indicated significant gains on the learning of concepts and practices relating to the large number of themes covered in the programme. The teachers liked the technology for training to large number at a distance.

Taleem Research Foundation (1999) evaluated the effectiveness of teacher training through teleconferencing for primary school teachers of District Primary Education Programme (DEP-DPEP) in the state of Tamil Nadu. The study revealed that majority of teachers were positive towards teleconference as a mode of training. The technology has the potential for training large number of teachers located at different sites. The quality of interaction among the teachers and the learners was reported to be high.

An experiment on Higher Cognitive Learning for the Engineering College Teachers by IIT Delhi was professionally evaluated on a pre-test, post-test format. Results showed that the post-test scores were higher than the pre-test. Participant's reaction was positive towards the course and the technology.

Classroom 2000+ was another experiment where lessons were telecast, palmtop computers and STD were used for feedback and interaction. Evaluation of the experiment showed that the technology could deliver quality education to remove existing disparity in education among different sections of the society. The findings of the study further revealed that in Physics and Maths the achievement of the experimental group was significantly higher than the control group. Mukhopadhyay and Parhar (1993), Panda (1998) and Goel (2000).

The Jhabua Development Communication Project, which was a satellite based interactive project, was evaluated both at the formative as well as the summative stage. A large number of educational institutes and research agencies were involved in the conduct of the research of JDCP. Over 40 studies have been conducted and well-documented reports are available. Continuous research is inbuilt in the system and evaluation studies are conducted regularly. Shah 1999 found that the percentage of viewers was around 37-38 per cent of the potential audience. The viewers were mainly male and more literate of the population. The reasons given by people for not viewing the TV programme was lack of time, lack of desire to engage in such activity and distances being too great to receive sites. SERVE (1998) found out that this project could promote general awareness among the villagers of Jhabua district.

Many organizations and institutions have used Interactive Television to train their workers. In the state of Gujarat, the adult education trainers were trained through satellite. National Productivity Council trained its senior technicians and supervisors. There were nine learning ends. Institution of Electronics and Telecommunication Engineering (IETE) located in Delhi trained a large number of engineers through interactive television. Extension workers were trained in Bhiwani district of the state of Haryana. All these experiments conducted were found to be effective as gave interactive experience to the participants.

The Indira Gandhi National Open University telecasts interactive sessions. Satellite communication with interactive mode of teaching is an additional input in some programmes. These programmes are mainly syllabus based. Teleconferencing has become a part of instructional system. According to Rao and Khan (1998), IGNOU used teleconferencing for approx 246 hours in 1995, 483 hours in 1996 and 495 hours in 1997. They reviewed the teleconferencing sessions conducted by

IGNOU over a period of three years. It was found that professional courses are appropriate for teleconferencing sessions, as learners in these courses are mature and motivated. IGNOU conducts the Extended Contact Programme (ECP) for students of Diploma in Higher Education. Sahoo (1994) conducted a study to access the teleconferencing experiment on PGDHE programme of IGNOU.

The focus of the study was from two angles:

1. Effectiveness of teleconferencing as a means of distance education, and
2. Teleconferencing as one of the components of extended contact programme (ECP).

Sahoos' study found the mode effective when used independently as well as in combination with other activities during ECP (brainstorming, discussion, and projects). Mishra (1999) conducted a study on teleconferencing at IGNOU. Mishra revealed a high degree of quality interaction between the learners and the resource persons. Majority of the time was devoted to interactions, which were related to the topics. The overall quality of teleconferencing was rated good to very good".

UGC conducted a two-way teleconferencing experiment in 1991 in collaboration with DECU, known as Talkback Experiment. Individual programmes were telecast and viewers could interact with the experts sitting at the studios. Kumari and Bose (2000), and Goel and Jaiswal (1992) found that students felt that CWC viewing must be made compulsory as part of the curriculum. Students found difficulty with language, format of programmes content and terminology used. The evaluation of the Talkback experiment reported by Panda (1992) indicated that in technical terms, the experiment was successful though more time was expected for talkback and for asking insightful and probing questions. The interaction needed to be multilingual rather than in English.

NIOS in collaboration with ISRO conducted a talkback experiment in 1996 with about 300 NIOS counselors of Gujarat State. Goel (2000) reports that the experiment was informative regarding NIOS.

Trivedi (1998) analysed various interactive satellite based experiments from 1991 to 1998. The main findings of the study were that the conceptual understanding of the participants improved significantly. The question-answer sessions were more effective than just viewing telecourses and interaction contributed to the knowledge gain of the participants. She concluded that inter-institutional co-operation was necessary for this system to be effective. Once the infrastructure is established, the operational costs are very low. In another comprehensive study Reddi (1996) analysed four teleconferencing experiments during 1991 to 1995. She concluded that there was no evidence to show that interaction through one-way video and two-way audio produced higher learning outcomes. Attendance to the programmes slowly decreased. Reddi also found favourable attitudes and reactions of participants towards teleconferencing.

Findings from the above review reveal that the teachers and students are favourable towards instructional television and administrators are more favourable towards ITV than the teachers. Students at all grade levels learn well from ITV though this is less true for older students than the younger ones. The studies also indicate that the effectiveness of ITV cuts across virtually all subjects.

The tremendous response to the interactive modality through telephone and fax in all these programmes indicates the trainees' enthusiasm and utilization of the media. These experiments started only in 1993, and the first evaluation of such programmes was held in 1996 and 1997.

Teleconferencing holds great promise. In most cases participation and response were found to be encouraging. Sessions were found to be quite effective in terms of learning outcomes and motivational level of the learners. Better planning and better pedagogic strategies are some of the key determinants of the success of TDCC (Rao and Khan 1998).

There are studies conducted on educational and interactive television in other developed and developing countries. The Asian Media Information and Communication (AMIC) studied the impact of television on the lives of children in Asia. Besides looking into the resources available for production of children's television programmes in Asia, the study examined the nature and type of children's television programmes available to them in Asia. AMIC conducted another study in 1999 on the portrayal of children in television. The survey showed the need to develop children's television in many countries in Asia. Seels et. al. (2001) in their review chapter on "Research on Learning from Television", published in the "Handbook of Research on Educational Communication and Technology" reviewed articles published in ERIC since 1966 and articles published in Psychology Abstracts since 1980s. The authors summarized that "as technologies become sophisticated, research on teaching, learning and technology has become complex. Interests have shifted to understanding how the process of teaching, learning and thinking are influenced by technologies. The shift from learning from media to learning with media has been welcome in emerging technologies".

Conclusion

Research can be a means of theory generation or a means for improving tools of development intervention. Fundamental research is used for theory generation whereas applied research facilitates and sharpens the tools of development intervention. Educational media, either broadcast or interactive, small or big, are essentially chosen for extending the outreach of education and improving the quality. From this very consideration, pressing of media into education is a developmental intervention. Hence, research in media has a clearly defined role. It is the domain of applied research and it should serve the purpose of research and development (R & D). To serve the purpose of improving effectiveness of educational media, research has several chartered areas, namely diagnosis of need, role of media for enhancing educational effectiveness, experimenting with alternative forms and combination of media to find optimal effectiveness, and evaluation of educational media to ensure its cost effectiveness, contribution to human learning, and more importantly informed technology choices.

Research on media, as reviewed here, only marginally contributes to these charters. For example, there are very few studies on the impact of media on student learning. Even if there are a few that indicate little or no impact of media on learning, such research has rarely, if ever, been followed up with alternative experimental variations on software format, organization of learning episodes, etc. depriving an opportunity to learn to fine tune use of media in education. Another major deficiency is the sophistication in the research methods and tools used. For example, very large number of studies in educational media border on 'audience research' that is concerned with viewers' reactions and preferences; and not necessarily the impact of programmes on viewers. As mentioned in the text, a large number of studies are devoted to reactions of students seeking their liking or disliking of the educational programmes and their perception about actual learning. Methodologically, it cannot stand the rigor that is necessary to design and implement media in education.

From a situation where educational media did not attract enough attention of the researchers, it has, however, come a long way to become an important subject of study. From the angle of quality, relevance and bearing upon the educational system, research on educational media has a long way to go and mature into an important tool for sharpening educational media.

7

Introduction to EDUSAT

Introduction

Educational television in India, as mentioned earlier, had its beginning in the early 1960s. One of the important landmarks was the SITE Experiment in early 1970s, exclusively on elementary education, that influenced later developments of educational media Classroom 2000+ was by far the first experiment in interactive television. A much larger leap was taken at the initiative of ISRO when it created DECU to experiment with interactive television for education and development with one-way video and two way audio interactivity. All these efforts led to the creation of a dedicated channel for education named Gyan Darshan.

The precursor to EDUSAT was contained in the National Action Plan for Inservice Education of Primary Teachers through distance education. It is in this document, for the first time that the concept of a nation-wide reception network for two-way video based learning was articulated. This was done as a follow up of E-9 Summit in Delhi in 1993. The documented was authored by Prof. Marmar Mukhopadhyay as UNESCO Consultant, funded by Asian Development Bank in 1996.

EDUSAT Vision and Missions

Conceptually, if National Action Plan was a seed, EDUSAT is a full grown tree with a massive vision. The title of the concept document, published by DECU is *"Educating the Nation: Need for a Dedicated Satellite"* (Mukhopadhyay, 2002). The vision of EDUSAT is most succinctly stated in the title itself, namely, *'Educating the Nation'*. Mukhopadhyay argued about the need for a dedicated satellite for continuing education of one billion people for creating a learning community which is necessary for India to emerge as a 'nation'.

This vision poses the challenge of transition from massive adult illiteracy for several million working children out of school coupled with huge drop out of children enrolled in elementary schools, poor performance at school and higher education, etc. to an educated nation marching ahead for a new place in the comity of nations. Mukhopadhyay provides a detailed diagnosis of the state of education in India.

The vision gets elaborated in a three dimensional mission-tapestry—educating people in and out of schools and colleges (formal, non-formal and open and distance education), education through ages (life-long learning) and education in the career (continuing education).

Before we move on to introducing the modality, it is important to mention how "educating the nation" agenda has been seen to be translated through the satellite based education. This is visible in the allocation of the 72 channels for achieving the three articulated missions. EDUSAT document proposes providing 28 channels each to school and higher education so that curricular programmes can be offered in various regional languages. Other channels are for language learning, culture, women's development, health, education of the senior citizens, toddlers, etc. Details of channel allocation are given in the appendix.

EDUSAT Modality

There are several dimensions in the modality of EDUSAT. The first and foremost is the educational aspect of the modality comprising content, pedagogy, and software including content generation. The second is the technology network, and the third is the management framework for EDUSAT.

Curricular Content

Educational television has normally been characterized by delivering enrichment programmed, at both school and higher education, the programmes delinked from curricular content and one-way broadcast has largely been responsible for non-utilization of educational television. There is an effort to correct this malady; in case of EDUSAT, emphasis has been placed much more pointedly on to programmes related directly to the prescribed curriculum of the concerned state boards of school education, and the universities. This will, hopefully, build the stakes of students enrolled in different kinds of programmes in the formal as well as nonformal and open and distance education institutions.

Pedagogy

On the issue of pedagogy, EDUSAT visualises creating a live virtual classroom. The main pedagogical proposition is to invite competent and effective teachers of different subjects into the studio at the teaching ends. With the teacher support material like Power Point presentations, computer graphics, animations, charts, models, etc. the expert teacher will present the curricular lesson that will be uplinked to the EDUSAT. The reception centres in various schools, colleges, and other educational institutions will be able to receive the presentation; students will also be able to ask questions and present their views within their own classroom settings. Such student communications will be uplinked to EDUSAT and downlinked into the teaching centre. The teacher shall be able to respond to such questions and comments, generating an interactive virtual classroom. This pedagogy is distinctly different from me broadcast pedagogy where prerecorded programmes are uplinked and broadcast.

The issues of software and content generation directly informed and influenced by the choice of the pedagogy, particularly the instructional design. In the proposed design of the pedagogy, the conventional software in the form of video programmes or CD-ROMs, either interactive or non-interactive, are not of particular importance. On the contrary, the expert presentations from the teaching ends are proposed to be recorded, digitized and archived facilitating retrieval by the learners according to their learning needs and convenience. The need and importance of conventional software is relevant only when such software can be used as teacher support material.

Technology Configuration

One of the important dimensions of EDUSAT is the technology configuration. There are two specific segments in technology configuration. One is the space segment which basically means provision of dedicated satellite. The second is the ground segment that is equipped with uplink facilities as well as reception facilities in different educational institutions and organizations.

The dedicated satellite was launched on 20 September, 2004 by ISRO. The first component of the ground segment is at the teaching ends with uplink facilities, usually with a studio and other associated facilities. Such facilities have been proposed to be installed at apex institutions at the national and state levels, universities and other such organizations that need to develop their own network for delivering education. The second component is the reception stations. Two kinds of reception facilities have been recommended – Satellite Interactive Terminal (SIT) and Receive only Terminal (RoT); have been proposed to be provided to the universities, colleges, senior secondary and secondary schools. Colleges include both general and professional colleges including teacher education institutions. RoT has been proposed be provided and installed in to elementary and primary schools. Given the number of existing educational institutions, the complete network should comprisd more than 1.2 million reception centres; about one million with RoT facilities, and remaining with SIT facilities.

Management

EDUSAT is not only a massive concept but also a colossal project for implementation and management. It has been proposed to constitute an EDUSAT management authority at the national and also at the state levels involving the government as well as different stakeholders.

Conclusion

The concept document on EDUSAT authored by Mukhopadhyay is dated June 2002. Subsequent to the concept document, there was a national consultation held in

NIEPA in 2003. The project document is dated 2004. Thus, the life of EDUSAT concept is more than three years.

As mentioned above, EDUSAT was launched in September 2004 – a year ago. There have been some preparations in establishing ground level network; some reception centres have also been activated. However, the programme delivery has not yet started though it may start any time. Instead of creating national and state authorities, EDUSAT is now being managed by a National Core Committee with its secretariat at IGNOU. The state of the art of development in EDUSAT has been dealt extensively by Mukhopadhyay (2005).

References and Bibliography

139th Report of HRD, (2004), Demands for Grants 2003-04 of the Department of Secondary and Higher Education, http://parliamentofindia.nic.in/rs/book2/reports/HRD/Report139th.html (accessed on 4/28/2004).

2002 Spacelink, Education Satellite, available at http://www.spacelink.org.uk/content/services/education-satellite.shtml (accessed on 10/21/2003)

2002 Spacelink, Welcome to the Spacelink Learning Foundation, 2003, available at http://www.spacelink.org.

Agarwal, B.C., (1988), *Message System Analysis of UGC Countrywide Classroom,* DECU, Ahmedabad, Space Application Centre.

Aghi Mira, (1996), Cited in "Television and Children: What Kids Are Viewing in Asia", Presentations by Aruna Goonasekera at International Forum of Researchers, *Young People and Media Tomarrow,* GREEM, Paris, 1997.

Agrawal, Binod, C., (1978), *Television Comes to Village – An Evaluation of SITE*; India Space Research Organization, Bangalore.

All India Radio, (1972), 'Listeners Research Unit' On-the Spot Investigation (Mimeo), Cuttack.

Antonysamy, (1989), *Teaching Environmental Concepts to School Dropouts Through Video and Charts*; M. Phil; Education, Madurai Kamaraj University.

Arularam I., (1990), *Evaluation of UGC's Countrywide Educational Television*, M. Phil, Education, Madurai Kamaraj University.

Arya Kavi, Krithivagan Saragawathi and Iyar Shyamala, (2005), Satellite-based Distance Education Programme at the Indian Institute of Technology Bombay, India in Reddi, Usha V. and Mishra Sanjaya (eds)., *Perspective on Distance Education Media in Asia*, COL, Vancouver.

Avam Arul I, (1989), *Evaluation of UGC Countrywide Education*; Department of Education; Madurai Kamraj University.

Beaming Education to the Nation, 2003, available at http://www.safrica.info/ess-info/sa-glance/education/mindset edu.html (accessed on 17/9/2004).

Bhaskaran, P., (1977), SITE for Children Morning Feedback; Space Application Centre, Ahmedabad, (Assisted by Ila Patel).

Biswal, B., (1980), *'Developing Strategies for Effective Utilization of School Broadcast Programme' in Orissa State;* Ph.D, MSU.

Biswal, B., (1980), *'Developing Strategies for Effective Utilization of School Broadcast Programme' in Orissa State;* Ph.D, MSU.

Central Institute of Educational Technology, (1975), A Study of the Functioning of School Broadcast Unit of AIR and a Case Analysis of Utilization of School Broadcast in Jaipur; NCERT, New Delhi.

CET, (1980), A Study into Utilization and Comprehensibility of School Television Programmes in Delhi, NCERT, New Delhi (mimeo).

Chakarvarty, T.R., and others, (1982), Satellite Instructional Television Experiment – A Study of Chattisgarh; Hyderabad, NIRD.

Chaudhari M.M., (1997), "The Limits and Challenges of Educational Technology in the Paradigm of Sustainable Development of India" in *Educational Technology 2000: A Global Vision for Open and Distance Learning* (Conference Papers); Singapore (August 15.17.1996), The Commonwealth of Learning, Vancouver, BC, Canada.

Chaudhary, S.S. and Bansal, K., (2000), "Interactive Radio Counseling in Indira Gandhi National Open University: A Study, *"Journal of Distance Education;* 15(2):37-51.

Chaudhary, Sohanvir S., (1991), *Teacher's Attitude Towards Schools Television and its Relationship with Mass Media Behavior and Job Satisfaction;* Ph. D. Thesis, University of Delhi, Delhi.

Christensen, P.R., (1985), The Radio Language Arts Project: Adapting the Radio Mathematics Model; Development Communication Report, Washington D.C; No. 49, USA.

Chu, G.C. and Schramm, (1987), *Learning from Television: What the Research Rays,* Stanford California, Institute for Communication Research.

Clark, R., (1994), Media will never Influence Learning; *Educational Technology Research and Development,* 45(4), 21-35.

Clark, Richard E., (2001), *Learning from Media;* Greenwich, CT: Information Age Publishers.

Das B.C. and Das, S., (2001), "Viewing Doordarshan Programme: Preferences on High School Students; *Indian Journal of Open Learning;* 10 (1-3); 100-109.

Dash, N.K., (1997), "Reactions of Primary School Teachers Towards Training through Interactive Television"; *Indian Journal of Open Learning;* 6(1&2);77-90.

Deodhar, P.S., (1991), *The Third Parent;* Vikas Publication, New Delhi.

Dewal O.S., (1997), Educational Technology in Fifth Survey of Educational Research, 1987-88, Trend Reports, NCERT, New Delhi.

Dhamija, N., (1985), *A Comparative Study of the Effectiveness of Three Approaches of Instructions – Conventional Radio Vision, and Modular Approach on Achievement of Students,* Ph.D Education, Kurukshetra University.

Doneriya, A., (1988), A Study of General Educational Television Programmes in Terms of Their Contents, Presentation, Students Reactions and Effectiveness, M.Ed. Dissertation, SOE, DAVV, Indore.

Educational Technology Programme, Government of India, Ministry of Human Resource Development, Department of Education, New Delhi, 1988.

EMPC IGNOU, (2005), Gyan Vani Gyan Darshan, June 2005, EMPC, IGNOU, New Delhi.

Goel D.R. (2000), MOS-DECU-ISRO Talkback Experiment in Goel, D.R. (ed) Educational Media in India. Bharatiya Kala Prakashan, Delhi.

Goel D.R., (1982), *A Study of School Broadcast in India;* Ph.D. Education, M.S. University.

Goel, D.R., (1985), *Educational Television in India: Organization and Utilization;* Department of Education, DAVV, Indore.

Goel, D.R., (2000), Indo – US Sub-Commission Project Classroom 2000+, in Goel, D.R. (ed.), *Educational Media in India*, Bharatiya Kala Prakashan, Delhi.

Goel, D.R., and Jaiswal Kiran, (1992), ISRO – UGC Talkback Experiment in India. *University News*, AIU, January, 1992.

Goodlad J.I., (1983), *A Place Called School*, McGraw – Hill, New York.

http://www.isro.org/rep2002/links/Geostationary.htm, (accessed on 10.10.2003)

Idayavani, S., (1991), 'Developing Video programme on Weathering and Work of the River' in *Physical Geography for Higher Secondary Students*; M. Phil, Education, Madurai Kamaraj University.

IGNOU, 2004, *IGNOU Profile 2004*, IGNOU, New Delhi.

IGNOU-NCERT, 2003, Distance Education Initiatives in District Primary Education Programme, DEP-DPEP, IGNOU, India.

ISRO, (2000), Development and Educational Communication Unit, Indian Space Research Organisation, Booklet, ISRO, India.

Joshi, I., (1987), *Content Analysis of Countrywide Classroom*, Ahmedabad: EMRC.

Kalimuthu, T., (1991), 'Developing a Video Programme on Environmental Pollution in *Biology for Higher Secondary Students*, M. Phil, Education, Madurai Kamaraj University

Kanade, H.M. (1982), *A Study of the Impact of Instructional Television on the Behaviour of the Rural School Children; Unpublished Doctoral Dissertation,* Baroda; M.S. University. Baroda.

Kasturirangan, K., (2003), Space Programme – India Forges Ahead. http://pib.nic.in/feature/feyr2001/fjan2001/f100120011.html.

Kulkarni, S.S. and Kapadia, G., (1974), 'Programmed Learning: Trend Report', in Buch, M.B. (ed.). *A Survey of Research in Education*, Baroda, IASE.

Kumar, K., (1978), *What Should Television Do for Rural Primary School?* NCERT, New Delhi and SAC, Ahmedabad (mimeo).

Kumari A. and Bose Vijaylaxmi, (1998), ISRO-DECU-IGNOU Talkback Experiment, 1994: A Report in Mohanty J. (ed.) Studies in Educational Broadcasting, Deep and Deep Publishers, New Delhi.

Maddu, V.M., (1978), *A Study of the Effectiveness of the Use of Motion Picture as Aids in the Teaching of Biological Science,* Osmania University.

Mangla, L.R., (1967), A Study of Comparative Achievement in Chemistry of the Tenth Class Students in TV and non-TV Schools, Unpublished Masters Thesis, JMI, New Delhi.

Ministry of Education, (1950), *The Report of the University Education Commission*, 1948-49, New Delhi, GOI Press.

Ministry of Education, (1956), *Report of the Secondary Education Commission*, Govt. of India, New Delhi.

Ministry of Education, (1966), Report of Education Commission: Education and National Development, New Delhi: GOI Press.

Ministry of Education, (1968), National Policy on Education, Ministry of Education, Government of India.

Ministry of Human Resource Development, (1986), *National Policy on Education;* New Delhi: MHRD.

Ministry of Human Resource Development, (1992), Programme of Action, New Delhi: MHRD.

Mishra, C.H.K. (1988), "Educational Technology: Trend Report" in Buch, M.B. (ed.), *Third Survey of Research in Education*, New Delhi, NCERT.

Mishra, S., (1999), "An Empirical Analysis of Interactivity in Teleconference"; *Indian Journal of Open Learning;* 8(3); 243-53.

Mody, B., (1978), Lessons from the Indian Satellite Experiment', *Educational Broadcasting International*, 11: (117-20).

Mohanty J., (1992), *Educational Technology*, Deep and Deep Publications, New Delhi.

Mohanty P.C., (1992), Mass Media and Education, Ashish Publishing House, New Delhi.

Mohanty S. and Behera S.C., (1986), Teacher Education in Programme under INSAT, *EFA Bulletin*, 8(1&2).

Mohanty, J. and Giri A.P., (1984), *An Evaluative Study of the School Broadcast Programme;* SCERT, Orissa.

Mohanty, J. and Sahu H.K., (1991), Country Wide Classroom Television Programmes: An Appraisal; *University News;* AIU; New Delhi; August 5.

Mohanty, J. and Seth, A., (1992), Evaluative Study of UGC Country Wide Television Programmes; *ASC Newsletter;* Utakal University.

Mohanty, J., (1992), Utilization of Community Wide TV Programmes: An Appraisal Study; *University News;* AIU; New Delhi; March.

Mohanty, J., and Rath A., (1990), Country Wide Classroom Television Programmes: An Appraisal Study; *University News;* AIU; New Delhi; December.

Mukhopadhyay Marmar, (2004), Evolution of Educational Technology in Mukhopadhyay Marmar (ed.), *Educational Technology: Knowledge Assessment*, Shipra, New Delhi.

Mukhopadhyay, M. and others (ed.), (1989), *Educational Technology: Year Book 1988*, New Delhi, AIAET.

Mukhopadhyay, M. and Parhar, M., (1993), Classroom 2000+: An Evaluative Study; New Delhi, AIAET (Commissioned by CIET).

Mukhopadhyaya Marmar and Sinha Neelam, (1983), Utilization of Media Facilities in Schools (An Evaluative Study of ET Scheme) NIEPA, New Delhi.

Nagaraju, C.S. and Ramkumar U., (1982), *School Broadcasting Utilization by High Schools in Bangalore District;* The Institute for Social and Economic Change, Bangalore.

Narayansamy, M., (1991), Enrichment of Vocabulary of Standard VI Students through Video; M. Phil; Education; Madurai Kamaraj University.

National Guidelines for Educational Broadcasting, (1983), National Guidelines for Educational Broadcasting, New Delhi: Ministry of Education and Culture, Government of India.

NCERT, (2005), National Curriculum Framework Review (2005), Systemic Reform, Volume II (Draft), NCERT, New Delhi.

Neurath, (1966)., *School Television in Delhi*, New Delhi, All India Radio.

Oberai, N., (1981), *Development and Evaluation of Radio Vision as an Instructional System;* Ph.D. Education; SG.

Panda, P.K., (1998), 'Feedback Report on Classroom 2000+' in Mohanty J. (ed.), *Studies in Educational Broadcasting Television and Radio;* Deep and Deep Publication; New Delhi.

Parhar, M., (1993), Impact of Media on Student Learning; Unpublished Doctoral Dissertation; New Delhi; Jamia Millia Islamia.

Parkash, Dharam and Lal, Harmesh, (1998), Using Satellite Technology for Special Orientation of Primary Teachers in Madhya Pradesh: A Study of Presentation Aspects and Production Values of Teleconferencing, Indian Journal of Open-Learning, 7(3):323-30.

Phutela R.L. (1998), Use of Interactive Television in the Orientation of Primary School Teachers, *Staff and Educational Development International* 2(1)35-41.

Phutela R.L., (2004), 'Satellites in Education' in Rajput J.S. (ed.), *Encyclopedia of Indian Education;* Vol. II; NCERT; New Delhi.

Phutela, R.L., (1980), *A Study into Utilization and Comprehensibility of School Television Programmes in Delhi, CIET, NCERT,* New Delhi.

Pillay Subramaniam G.S., (1992), Management of Educational Technology in Tamil Nadu: A Project Sponsored by NIEPA, New Delhi, Department of Education, Madurai Kamraj University.

Programme of Action, National Policy on Education (1986), Government of India, Ministry of Human Resource Development, Department of Education, New Delhi, 1992.

Rao, V.R. and Khan, Zeba, (1988), "Satellite Based Interactive Learning System at IGNOU: Retrospect and Prospects." Paper presented at International Conference on Collaborative Networked Learning, IGNOU (16-18 February, 1988), New Delhi.

Reddi Usha V. and Mishra Sanjaya (ed.), (2005), *Perspectives on Distance Education: Educational Media in Asia;* Commonwealth of Learning, Vancouver

Reddi, Usha V., (1996), Learning from the Application of Communication Technology in Higher Education in India, In Educational Technology 2000: A Global Vision for Open and Distance Learning, Commonwealth of Learning (1997), Vancouver BC, Canada.

Reddi, Usha V., (1997), "Lessons from the Applications of Communication Technology in Higher Education." In *Educational Technology 2000: A Global Vision for Open and Distance Learning* (Conference Papers), Singapore (August 15-17, 1996). The Commonwealth of Learning, Vancouver, B.C. Canada.

Reddi, Usha V., (2003), *Educational Broadcasting in the Commonwealth with Special Reference to Educational Television*, CEMCA, New Delhi.

Rehman, S., (1977), A Study in Educational Television; Department of Education; Ministry of Education and Social Welfare, New Delhi.

Report, (1989), Use of Satellite Services for Education, New Delhi, (mimeo).

Richstad J. and McMillan M., (1978), Mass Communication and Journalism in the Pacific Islands : A Bibliography: University Press of Hawaii, Hawaii.

Roy, B., (1974), *A Study of the Cognitive Effects of ETC Programmes Broadcast by the Delhi TV Centre;* New Delhi; NCERT.

Sahoo, P.K., (1994), 'Teleconferencing in Distance Education: IGNOU Experiment', *Indian Journal of Open Learning*, 3(1), 29-32.

Sambooram, K.V., (1980), *The Impact of Television Viewing on Achievement in History and Tamil;* M.Ed. Dissertation; Madras University, Madras.

Saravanan M., (1990), Improving the Quality of UGC's Countrywide Classroom Project, Unpublished Report on Educational Broadcasting Radio and Television, Department of Education, Madurai.

SCERT, (1982), *On the Spot Evaluative Study on School Broadcast Programmes in the Towns of Cuttack and Bhubaneswar;* SCERT; Bhubaneswar.

Schramm, W.L., (1977), *Big Media, Little Media: Tools and Technologies for Instruction*, Sage, London.

Seels Barbara, Berry Lousistt, Fullerton K., Horn Launa J., (2001), "Research on Learning from Television" in Jonassen David H., (ed), *Handbook of Research for Educational Communications and Technology*, Lawrence Erlbaum Associates Publishers, New Jersy.

SERVE, (1988), An Evaluative Study of Knowledge Gains in Interactive Training Programme of JDCP in Jhabua District, Society for Education, Research and voluntary Efforts, Jaipur.

Seth, Indu, (1983), A Study of the Effectiveness of Educational Television on the Educational Development of Primary School Children; Ph.D. Education, M.S. University, Baroda.

Shah, G.B., Mehta, S.J. and Kulkarni, S.S., (1978), 'Educational Technology, A Trend Report in Buch M.B. (ed.) *Second Survey of Research in Education;* Baroda; SERD, 1978.

Shah, M.C., (1972), *The Scope, Utility and Limitation of Educational Television in India;* Ph.D. Thesis; M.S. University; Baroda.

Sharma, R.C., (2002), "Interactive Radio Counseling in Distance Education," *University News*, 40(10):8-12.

Shukla, S. and K. Kumar, (1977), Impact of SITE on Primary School Children; Technical Report, ISRO-SAC-TR-09-78; New Delhi, NCERT.

Shukla, S., (1991), 'Research in Educational Technology: A Trend Report' in Buch, M.B. (ed), *Fourth Survey of Research in Education;* New Delhi; NCERT.

Sindhi, J.N., (1963), *A Study of the Provisions Prevailing and the Use being Made of Television in the Teaching of Hindi to Class X of Delhi Higher Secondary Schools in 1962-63;* Unpublished Master's Thesis; University of Delhi, Delhi.

Singh J. and Umare J.S., (1986), Report on ETV Utilization in Maharashtra CIET; NCERT, New Delhi.

Singh J., Prasad S., Bajpai A. and Kaur R.J., (1984), Pre-telecast Teaching of the ETU Programmes – Some Observations, New Delhi, CIET, NCERT.

Singh, J. and Singh A.K., (1983), *Report on ETV Utilization in Orissa;* CIET, NCERT, New Delhi.

Space Today Online, 2003, China's Spacecraft, available at http://www.spacetoday.org/China/Chinasatellites.html (accessed on 4/23/2004).

Space Today Online, 2004, Japan: One of the First Space faring Nations available at http://www.spacetoday.org/Japan/History.html (accessed on 4.23.2004).

Sudama, G.P. and Goel D.R., (1988), A Study of School Broadcasts in Baroda District, The Majaraja Sayajirao University of Baroda, Baroda.

Sukumar, B., (2001), "IGNOU Interactive Radio Counseling: A Study"; *Indian Journal of Open Learning;* 10(I); 81-92.

Taleem Research Foundation (1999), Assessing the Effectiveness of Teleconferencing System of DEP-DPEP Programmes in Tamil Nadu, Ahmedabad.

Towards an Enlightened and Human Society, 1990, NPE, 1986 – A Revision, New Delhi.

Trivedi, Bela, (1998), *Network Utilization by User Agencies in Training and Development Communication Channel in India;* Indian Space Research Organization, Ahmedabad.

Trivedi, Bela, 2005, Teleconferencing in India: Rural Development in COL, CEMCA, *Teleconferencing A Training Kit*, CEMCA, New Delhi.

UNESCAP, 2004, available at http://www.unescap.org/icstd/SPACE/documents/telehealth/nasda.asp.

UNESCO (1996), Inservice Education of Primary Teachers: Application of Interactive Television, New Delhi; UNESCO.

Usha Chander and Sharma R.C. (2003), "Bridges to Effective Learning Through Radio," *International Review of Research in Open and Distance Learning*, April 2003. http://www.irrodl.org/content/sharma-research.html.

Index